D0138544

J 973 .0496 STU V.1
Student almanac of
African American history
/

PALM BEACH COUNTY
LIBRARY SYSTEM
3650 SUMMIT BLVD.
WEST PALM BEACH, FLORIDA 33406

Student Almanac of African American History

Volume 1: From Slavery to Freedom, 1492–1876

Student Almanac of African American History

Volume 1: From Slavery to Freedom, 1492–1876

GREENWOOD PRESS
Westport, Connecticut • London

Library of Congress Cataloging-in-Publication Data
Media Projects, Inc.
Student almanac of African American history.
          p. cm—(Middle school reference)
          Includes bibliographical references and index.
ISBN: 0–313–32596–0 (set: alk. paper)—ISBN: 0–313–32597–9 (v. 1)—
ISBN: 0–313–32598–7 (v. 2)
     1. African Americans—History—Miscellanea—Juvenile literature. 2. African
Americans—History—Sources—Juvenile literature. 3. Almanacs, American—Juvenile
literature. I. Series.
E185.S897 2003
973'.0496073—dc21   2002035332

British Library Cataloguing in Publication Data is available.

Copyright © 2003 by Greenwood Publishing Group, Inc.

All rights reserved. No portion of this book may be
reproduced, by any process or technique, without the
express written consent of the publisher.

Library of Congress Catalog Card Number: 2002035332

ISBN: 0–313–32596–0 (set)
          0–313–32597–9 (vol. 1)
          0–313–32598–7 (vol. 2)

First published in 2003

Greenwood Press, 88 Post Road West, Westport, CT 06881
An imprint of Greenwood Publishing Group, Inc.
www.greenwood.com

Printed in the United States of America
(∞)™
The paper used in this book complies with the
Permanent Paper Standard issued by the National
Information Standards Organization (Z39.48–1984).

10 9 8 7 6 5 4 3 2 1

A Media Projects, Inc. Production
Contributing Writers: Helene Avraham, Beverly Vallencourt, Carolyn Jackson
Design: Amy Henderson
Production: Anthony Galante and Jim Burmester
Editors: Helene Avraham and Carter Smith
Copy Editor: Beth Wilson
Indexer: Marilyn Flaig

CONTENTS

Volume 1: From Slavery to Freedom, 1492–1876

Introduction: From Slavery to Freedom, 1492–1876 7

Chapter One   Unwilling Immigrants: Slavery in Colonial America,
1492–1763 11

Chapter Two   That All Men Are Created Equal:
Slavery in Revolutionary America, 1764–1820 37

Chapter Three   The Road to War: The Antebellum Era,
1821–1860 65

Chapter Four   Free at Last: The Civil War and Reconstruction,
1861–1876 97

Glossary 127

Resources 131

Selected Bibliography 137

Index 139

From Slavery to Freedom
1492–1876

"Is not the slave trade entirely at war with the heart of man? And surely that which is begun by breaking down the barriers of virtue, involves in its continuance destruction to every principle, and buries all sentiments in ruin! When you make men slaves, you… compel them to live with you in a state of war."

—Olaudah Equiano, who escaped from slavery in colonial America

In 1505, Portuguese traders kidnapped 17 Africans and sent them in chains across the Atlantic Ocean. They then sold them as slaves on the Caribbean island of Hispaniola. In some ways, that voyage marks the beginning of what we call African American history.

Over the course of the 300 or so years that followed the arrival of those first enslaved Africans in the Caribbean, millions more Africans were captured and sent to the Americas. Although as many as half of those captured died of disease or hunger before reaching the Americas, at least 8 or 9 million survived the voyage. *Student Almanac of African American History* is about those people and their descendants.

No one could have predicted the incredible strength that those early Africans would demonstrate in the Americas. But the story of slavery is only part of the story of African American history. As you will read, African

Americans not only survived despite the long history of slavery. They have also created a unique and rich culture that has shaped the history of all Americans.

This first volume of *Student Almanac of African American History* tells the story of the struggle against slavery in what would become the United States, from its beginnings to the end of the **Civil War** (see p. 108). It also describes the ways in which enslaved Africans and free African Americans alike created new lives for themselves and, in the process, remade America itself.

SLAVERY IN COLONIAL AMERICA

The first chapter covers how slavery first came to the Americas with early Spanish and Portuguese explorers. Most of this chapter's story, though, takes place in Great Britain's 13 colonies. That part of the story began in Jamestown, Virginia, in 1619. It was in that year that the first 20 Africans were sold to **Jamestown** colonists (see p. 25).

In this chapter, readers will learn how slavery went from being a cruel act done to individual Africans to become a way of life that governments protected with laws. For example, in the earliest colonies, wealthy landowners or businessmen kept **indentured servants** (see p. 25). Some servants were white Europeans. Others were black Africans. After working for a time for a landowner or businessman, white servants were free to start new lives. However, African servants were not treated the same way. In 1663, a Virginia court ruled that any child born to an African servant was automatically a servant as well. This meant that African servants were slaves for life.

AFRICAN AMERICANS AND REVOLUTIONARY AMERICA

By the late 1700s, many people in the British colonies had grown tired of being asked to pay taxes to the British government without having someone of their choosing represent them in the British government. Many of these colonists thought that this was unfair. At the same time, all 13 British colonies allowed slavery. Many African Americans—both free and enslaved—felt angry that white patriots spoke of being enslaved by the British king, without questioning keeping Africans as slaves. When the **American Revolution** (see p. 47) began, many African Americans were inspired by the call for freedom.

In this chapter, you will learn about how African Americans fought for their freedom during the American Revolution. This chapter also covers the debate on slavery during and after the war. Readers will learn about how the first version of the **Declaration of Independence** (see p. 53) called for an end to slavery, and why that passage was taken out of the final draft. You will also learn about the infamous "Three-Fifths Compromise" in the **U.S. Constitution** (see p. 62), which counted each enslaved African as three-fifths of a person.

The chapter also describes how a simple invention called the **cotton gin** (see p. 51) would help spread slavery across the South by making it possible to grow and harvest cotton from South Carolina to Mississippi and beyond. But opening all this land to cotton fields came with a price. Picking all the crops that the cotton gin allowed landowners to grow required many more enslaved Africans to perform the work.

Not all African Americans in the early years of the United States were enslaved. Chapter 2 also discusses the lives of important **free blacks** (see p. 23), such as **Richard Allen** (see p. 46), who helped found the **African Methodist Episcopal Church** (see p. 46) in Philadelphia. You will learn about **Paul Cuffe** (see p. 52), a successful businessman, who helped organize a movement to colonize Great Britain's West African colony of Sierra Leone. Also included is the story of African American participation in the **War of 1812** (see p. 62), between the United States and Great Britain.

The Road to Civil War

By the early 1800s, most states in the North had decided to make slavery illegal. Meanwhile, Southern states fought to protect their right to hold slaves. As the country grew, supporters and opponents of slavery fought about whether slavery should be allowed in the new western territories. Beginning in 1820, when the U.S. Congress passed the **Missouri Compromise** (see p. 58), the federal government worked to balance the number of free states with the number of slave states.

Chapter 3 of *Student Almanac of African American History* is partly about those government compromises. It is also about heroic African

Americans such as **Harriet Tubman** (see p. 89), **Frederick Douglass** (see p. 80), and **Sojourner Truth** (see p. 89), among others, who saw no way to compromise over freedom and fought to free enslaved African Americans.

CIVIL WAR AND RECONSTRUCTION

In the end, compromise failed. In 1861, most of the slaveholding states of the South decided to leave the United States and create a new country called the **Confederate States of America** (see p. 110). For five years, the **U.S. Civil War** (see p. 108) tore the nation apart. During the war, President **Abraham Lincoln** (see pp. 85, 119) signed a law called the **Emancipation Proclamation** (see p. 113), freeing all enslaved African Americans in the Confederate states.

When the war ended, enslaved Africans everywhere in the United States and its territories were free. For a dozen years, during a period of **Reconstruction** (see p. 123), it appeared that African Americans might have a fair share of life in the United States. But by 1877, the old forces had regained their power. African Americans might be free, but they were still a class apart. The struggle for economic and political power began again. That struggle is the topic of Volume 2 of this series.

HOW TO USE THIS BOOK

Each chapter in *Student Almanac of African American History* is composed of two parts. The first part is a short essay that gives a summary of the major events in that time in African American history. The second part is an A–Z section that describes many important people, events, and terms that have to do with the time period.

To help readers find related ideas more easily, many terms are cross-indexed. Within both the essay and A–Z section of each chapter, some words appear in **bold letters**, followed by a page number. That means the term is also a separate A–Z entry in the book which should be read for more information. Other unfamiliar words are printed in ***bold italics***. Short definitions of these words can be found in a glossary that begins on page 126. Finally, words that may be hard to pronounce are followed by a pronunciation key.

CHAPTER ONE

Unwilling Immigrants

Slavery in Colonial America, 1492–1763

"At the time we came into this ship, she was full of black people, who were all confined in a dark and low place, in irons. … [M]any of us died every day. … When our prison could hold no more, the ship sailed."

—Slave story about the Middle Passage

There are some who believe that the first Africans to arrive in the Americas came as early as 800 BCE. These early explorers may have made contact with the Olmecs, an ancient civilization living in what is now Mexico. Although we can't prove this, we do know that Africans took part in the European exploration that began with the arrival of Christopher Columbus in 1492. The first African whose arrival is recorded was an enslaved man named **Estevanico** (*es-tay-vah-NEE-koh*) (see p. 22). He arrived in 1527 with a Spanish party of 400 people. Estevanico crossed the Southwest to Mexico. He was sold to the Spanish governor and later killed while acting as a scout.

EUROPEANS AND THE AFRICAN SLAVE TRADE

Humans have practiced slavery throughout their history. Ancient societies throughout Europe, Asia, and Africa enslaved people they captured in war. As early as 900 CE, Muslim traders from North Africa captured Africans from south of the Sahara. They sold them into slavery in Asia and Europe. (See **Leo Africanus**, p. 21.) During this time, most enslaved people were eventually freed. Some **African kingdoms** (see p. 19), such as the Kingdom of Benin, are known to have enslaved prisoners captured in war for use in agriculture or mining. Also, the children of enslaved parents did not automatically become enslaved. In the Americas—the New World to Europeans—slavery did not involve only prisoners captured in war. It also became a business based on human property.

Standards of living in Europe and Africa had been about equal for hundreds of years. In the 15th century, however, European technology moved ahead. The Europeans began to manufacture different types of goods. Then, during the 16th century, Europeans began taking lands in Asia, Africa, and the Americas. They needed people to work the mines and plantations they were developing in these growing empires. They persuaded some Africans to capture their enemies and sell them as slaves. In exchange the Africans got guns, beads, mirrors, and other goods not made in Africa. This happened mostly in West Africa, where there were ports on the Atlantic Ocean, closest to Europe and the Americas. West Africans had a tradition of working for other peoples. However, they had no idea that once they became enslaved, they would never see their homelands again.

The Portuguese began the slave trade by selling enslaved Africans to work plantations set up on the Madeiras (*muh-DEER-uhs*) and Canary Islands near the African coast. These were the first to rely on African slave labor. Later the plantation system would spread across Latin America and the American South.

Timeline

1492

Pedro Alonzo Niño, reported to be a black man, navigates Christopher Columbus's *Santa Maria*.

1502

Portugal lands the first shipload of enslaved Africans in the Western Hemisphere.

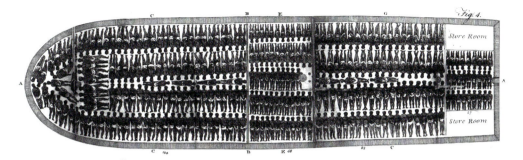

This diagram of a slave ship shows how tightly Africans were packed into ships. (Library of Congress)

As the slave trade grew, enslaved Africans were sold to Spanish landowners in the Caribbean and to Portuguese landowners in Brazil. Soon the Portuguese slave traders had competition from the French, Dutch, and English. Before it ended, the slave trade took 50 million people from Africa.

A FORCED JOURNEY TO THE AMERICAS

After they were captured, the Africans were brought to the West African coast. There slave traders bid and bargained for this human merchandise. Natives of Senegal brought the highest prices because they were often skilled in crafts. Other desirable Africans came from Gambia, the Gold Coast, and Guinea (see map, p. 35). Some peoples made themselves less sought-after. The Ibos from Calabar developed a reputation for suicide. The Congolese people were said to be weak.

1513	1517	1607	1619
Thirty Africans accompany Vasco Núñez de Balboa when he discovers the Pacific Ocean.	**Bartolomé de Las Casas** appeals to Spain to replace Native American labor with African labor.	English establish a colony at **Jamestown**, Virginia.	A Dutch ship brings the first 20 enslaved Africans to Jamestown, Virginia.

After the bidding, the Africans were loaded onto waiting ships. The journey from West Africa to the Americas took many weeks. Historians believe that at least 20 percent of the captured Africans died on the voyage to the Americas. It is certain that thousands died on the voyages across the Atlantic Ocean known as **The Middle Passage** (see p. 30). During these journeys, enslaved peoples were treated like cargo and forced to bear horrible conditions. Slave traders were interested only in the high profits they could make. Human African cargo became known as "black gold."

A profitable **"triangle trade"** (see p. 34) developed. One triangle involved bringing enslaved peoples from Africa to the **West Indies** (see p. 35) and depositing them for sale. Then molasses made by slave labor was picked up and brought to northeast America. In America, rum was made from the molasses and shipped back to Africa to be traded for more slaves. A second triangle involved carrying manufactured goods from Europe to northeast America, where they were deposited for sale or *barter*. Raw lumber was loaded onto the ship before it sailed for the Indies. Islanders needed lumber because all the trees had been cut down to make room for sugarcane. Traders sold the lumber and picked up sugar to take back to Europe (see map, p. 34).

SLAVERY IN NORTH AMERICA

Europeans brought enslaved Africans to the Americas to fill a labor shortage. Native Americans resisted enslavement. They had little to gain

1623	1641	1655	1664
William Tucker, born in Jamestown, Virginia, becomes the first black child born in the English colonies.	Massachusetts becomes the first British colony to legalize slavery by statute through its **Massachusetts Body of Liberties**.	Enslaved African **Elizabeth Key** wins her freedom in a Virginia court. Her victory is due to an English law that said that if a child's father is free, then the child should also be free.	The English defeat the Dutch and take New Netherland. The colony is renamed New York. The name of the colony's capital is also changed—from New Amsterdam to New York City.

from laboring on European farms and could escape into the wilderness. Even so, thousands of Native Americans died of diseases, such as smallpox, that were carried by the colonists. Some white **indentured** (*in-DEN-churd*) **servants** came from Europe (see p. 25). These servants were working-class people who agreed to work for a master for a few years in exchange for passage to America. While in service to one master, they could be sold to another, the same as an African servant could. However, once an indentured servant's term of service to his master was over, he was free to leave and make his own life for himself. However, not enough white indentured servants came from Europe to fill the labor shortage.

Europeans who invested in the American colonies for profit worried they would lose money. Then in 1619, a Dutch trader sold about 20 Africans to a merchant in the Virginia colony of **Jamestown** (see p. 25). These were the first Africans sold in an English American colony. More soon followed. The 13 colonies proved a good market. Wealthy people in all the colonies bought enslaved Africans. Slave labor was especially welcome on southern plantations where rice, tobacco, and indigo, a plant used to make dye, were grown.

Turning Africans into a slave class took effort. Often traders "seasoned" their human cargo on sugarcane plantations in the Caribbean. Cane grew fast on the hot, humid islands. Slaves were cruelly whipped to harvest the cane and grind it into molasses. After this experience, it was assumed they would be grateful to work in English North America.

1670　　1672　　1688　　1693

After a free African American named **Anthony Johnson** dies, a Virginia court takes his land away from his family. A colonial jury decides that African Americans could not own land.

The **Royal African Company** is established and soon controls the transatlantic slave trade.

Mennonites from **Germantown**, Pennsylvania, write the first formal protest against slavery in the Western Hemisphere.

Boston clergyman **Cotton Mather** organizes the Society of Negroes in Massachusetts, the earliest known African American religious meeting.

For slaves, life in the New England and middle Atlantic colonies was not quite as difficult as in the Caribbean. Some slaveowners eventually freed their enslaved Africans. However, laws were written that made escape from slavery hard. For example, one part of **The Articles of Confederation of the United Colonies of New England** (see p. 21), written in 1643, said that any enslaved African escaping from one New England colony to another would have to be returned.

On southern plantations, life was harder. Historians know this from reading written documents. One good example is the diary of Virginia planter **William Byrd II** (see p. 22). Some southern slaveholders were less brutal than the Spanish and Portuguese, but they were far less likely to free their slaves.

FREE AFRICAN AMERICANS

From the beginning, some people objected to slavery. Others protested that slave labor was needed in order for the American economy to survive. African Americans were easier to keep enslaved. Unlike Europeans and Native Americans, they had only tiny communities to which they could flee and mingle with the population. The colonists made sure that even free Africans were denied full citizenship by writing laws called **black codes** (see p. 22) that controlled their behavior. One historian wrote, "**Free blacks** [see p. 23] were often educated in segregated schools, punished in

1715	1722	1723	1735
North Carolina officially recognizes slavery as legal. Although no North Carolina laws before this time had made slavery illegal, this was the first time the colony officially declared it legal.	South Carolina **"black code"** law states that a slave owner who frees a slave must provide transportation out of the colony for the freed person. If a freed slave is found in the colony after one year, he or she will be enslaved once again.	Virginia's House of Burgesses passes a law that states that free African Americans are not permitted to vote or carry weapons.	Georgia passes an act prohibiting the importation of slaves.

segregated prisons, nursed in segregated hospitals, and buried in segregated cemeteries."

Nevertheless, a few hardy free African Americans survived and succeeded. They were most likely to find jobs in the cities of the Deep South, such as New Orleans, Charleston, Mobile, and Pensacola. They worked as carpenters, *masons*, mechanics, and tailors. Some married local white people of French ancestry. Their children became known as **Creoles** (*CREE-oles*). A very few free blacks became landowners and bought enslaved peoples themselves. Life was tougher in the North, but in Boston, New York, and Philadelphia there were also more paid jobs available for Africans. Women worked as household servants. Men found work as skilled and unskilled laborers. Life was hardest for free Africans in the upper southern states of Virginia, Tennessee, and Maryland. There, they often worked alongside enslaved peoples on farms and in factories. In Baltimore, free Africans were poorer than in most colonial cities.

Nowhere was life easy. True freedom was rare in colonial America. Laws forbade all women—slave or free, white or African—to own their own property. They could not even keep money from working, since their husbands, fathers, or other male guardians could claim the pay for themselves. Some white men were indentured servants, willing to work for a number of years for a master before gaining freedom. They could also be forced to serve in the British navy. White and black servants could be bought and sold, whipped and

1739

In one of the earliest major slave revolts in the British colonies, a group of enslaved Africans attempt to escape from Stono, South Carolina, to Spanish Florida. The colonial militia stops the rebels. During the clash, at least 20 whites and more slaves are killed.

1744

A "Negro School House" is opened in Charleston, South Carolina, by Alexander Garden, an English missionary, with two educated slaves as teachers. The school continues in operation until 1764.

1749

Under pressure from plantation owners, Georgia repeals the laws prohibiting the importation of slaves.

1756–1763

Britain and France wage war in North America in the conflict known as the **French and Indian War**, or the Seven Years' War. Both free and enslaved African Americans serve in the war on the British side, although mainly as unarmed laborers.

forced to work in the fields. If they survived their required service, white men were freed and might eventually prosper. Never did they face the threat, as Africans did, that their children would become their master's property and their families could be torn apart. Eventually, as colonial society developed, servants with white skin were treated better.

Thus, in colonial times, slavery was in conflict with the human values for which the English colonists said they stood. American leaders said they stood for liberty and freedom, but they treated African Americans quite differently.

1758 | 1758 | 1762

African Baptist Church, the first black **Baptist** church in the United States, is erected on **William Byrd's** Virginia plantation.

Quakers prohibit slavery among their members.

Virginia enacts a law that excludes African American males from voting and gives suffrage only to white men.

A-Z of Key People, Events, and Terms

African art and culture (to the 1500s)

African art through the 16th century was rich and varied. In general, Africans created works that were used for daily life and in religion. In West Africa, the region from which most African Americans came, craftsmen created beautiful pieces of sculpture and pottery. Weavers wove complex patterns on baskets and in cloth. Many artists worked with material, such as wood and cloth, that do not age well over the centuries. Therefore, only a few examples from early periods exist. Pieces from sturdy material have survived. For example, archaeologists have found bronze sculptures from Benin and *terra-cotta* figures from Mali. (See **African kingdoms**, below.)

Highly skilled artists from Benin created bronze sculptures. (Private collection)

Most early African societies had no written language. Professional storytellers, called "*griots*" *(GREE-ohs)*, memorized histories, folktales, and proverbs. Villages hired griots to entertain and teach their communities. In time, the Islamic religion brought writing to some of these villages. In those societies, some of these histories and stories were written in Arabic.

Music and dance were also important to Africans. African musicians used stringed and percussion instruments as well as their voices to perform. When the slave trade to America began, enslaved Africans brought the art and music they knew with them. In America, they made pottery having African designs. They created stringed instruments and played African music. Many musical and art forms that are today considered "American" can be traced to their African roots. Among these are blues, jazz, and rock and roll.

African kingdoms

Throughout its history, Africa has been home to powerful empires as well as smaller civilizations. West Africa had three large civilizations and many smaller ones. The three most important kingdoms were Ghana (ca. 300 CE–1076), Mali (ca. 1200 CE–1500), and Songhai (1464 CE–1591).

The Kingdom of Ghana was located along the Senegal and upper Niger rivers. Much of it lay in what is today the nation of Mali. Ghana gained wealth and power through its control of the gold and salt trades. At its height, the kingdom supported scholars, a powerful army, and a large population. In 1076, Muslims from the north invaded Ghana. The invasion began the decline of the Kingdom of Ghana and the start of the Mali Empire.

The Mali Empire grew to be larger than Ghana. It was also wealthier and more powerful. The empire's rulers made Islam the state religion. Yet, many people who lived far from the capital city continued to practice traditional **religions** (see p. 32). Mansa Musa, Mali's most famous emperor, made a religious journey

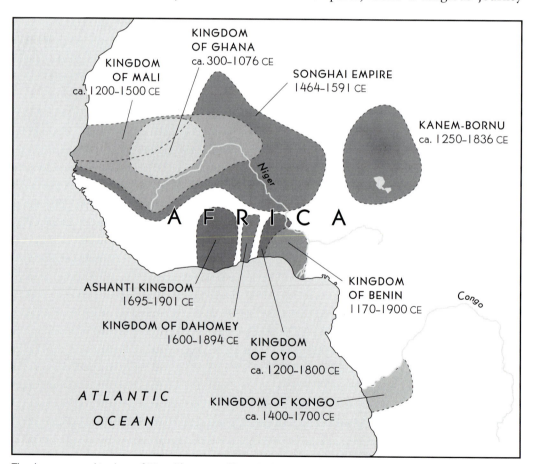

The three greatest kingdoms of West Africa were Ghana, Mali, and Songhai. The map above also shows many of the other important West African kingdoms.

called a pilgrimage, to *Mecca*, in 1324. (Mecca, in modern Saudi Arabia, is the most holy site in Islam.) On his journey, Mansa Musa took more than 8,000 servants, 500 slaves, and 100 camels, each carrying 300 pounds of gold.

The Songhai (*song-GUY*) Empire rose to power under the leadership of Sunni Ali Ber (*SUN-nee ahl-EE BAYR*). He led the Songhai army to victory against Mali in 1468. Sunni Ali did not accept Islam. He supported traditional religions and cultures of the region.

The empire's next strong emperor was Askia Muhammad (*AHS-kee-uh mu-HAH-muhd*). He made Islam the official religion of Songhai. The city of Timbuktu (*tim-buk-TOO*) rose as a center of Islamic learning. Large universities grew in Timbuktu and other cities in the empire.

A number of smaller West African kingdoms rose and fell during this period. These kingdoms included Dahomey (*dah-HOM-ee*), Benin (*ben-EEN*), and Asante (*as-AHN-te*), among others. (Also see **African Art and Culture**, p. 19.)

Africanus, Leo

Leo Africanus was born el Hasan ben Muhammed el-Wazzan-ez-Zayyati (*ha-SAHN ben mu-HAH-muhd WAH-zen ez-zay-AH-tee*) in 1485. He was born in the Muslim-controlled city of Granada, Spain. After Spain conquered Granada, his family moved to Morocco in North Africa. El Hasan was a Muslim. He began traveling throughout Africa and the Arab world. In 1518 he was captured by Italian pirates. They presented him to Pope Leo X. The pope granted el Hasan his freedom and baptized him "Johannis Leo de Medici." He became better known as "Leo Africanus." The pope gave him a job teaching Arabic and African history. In 1550 Leo wrote a book titled *Description of Africa*. It became the best account of Africa available to Europeans for several centuries.

The Articles of Confederation of the United Colonies of New England

In 1643, representatives of the colonies of Massachusetts Bay, Plymouth, Connecticut, and New Haven met in Boston. They formed a group called the United Colonies of New England. The colonies promised to defend each other from attacks by Native Americans. One clause of the Confederation's constitution was important for African Americans. It said that the United Colonies agreed to return runaway enslaved peoples or servants to their masters. This cooperation among the New England colonies made escape from slavery difficult. Future fugitive slave laws were based on this clause.

Black Codes

Black codes were laws that controlled the behavior of free blacks. The codes included laws that forbade African Americans to carry weapons, meet in groups, and testify in court. Laws having to do with enslaved African Americans were called slave codes.

Byrd, William II

Born in Virginia in 1674, William Byrd II inherited his father's plantation and its many enslaved Africans. Byrd was a highly educated man, but he lacked compassion for the Africans who worked his plantation. The punishments he gave out were often cruel. Byrd kept a secret diary that detailed life on his plantation. Historians have learned much about life on plantations from this diary.

Estevanico

Estevanico (*es-tay-vah-NEE-koh*), also known as Esteban, was born in Morocco. Portuguese slave traders captured him in 1513. He was sold to a Spaniard. In 1527, Estevanico and his master joined an expedition to explore and conquer lands in Florida for Spain. The expedition failed. Estevanico was one of only four men who were left alive. This group made their way across what is today the U.S. Southwest. One of the men, Alvar Núñez Cabeza de Vaca, kept a diary of the journey. De Vaca noted that Estevanico served as the group's translator and negotiator with Native Americans. De Vaca wrote that Estevanico "was constantly in conversation, finding out about routes, towns, and other matters we wished to know." Estevanico became known as a healer among the Native Americans in the region. The group traveled for nearly ten years before reaching Mexico City in 1536.

A Colonial Slave Owner's Diary (1709–1711)

William Byrd II owned a plantation in Virginia on which a number of enslaved African Americans worked. The secret diary he kept offers a look at eighteenth-century plantation life. In these excerpts Byrd mentions Jenny and Eugene, two of his slaves.

February 8, 1709. I rose at 5 o'clock this morning and read a chapter in Hebrew and 200 verses in Homer's *Odyssey*. I ate milk for breakfast. I said my prayers. Jenny and Eugene were whipped. I **danced my dance**. I read law in the morning and Italian in the afternoon. . . .

◀ **danced my dance**
an exercise Byrd did

June 10, 1709. I rose at 5 o'clock this morning but could not read anything because of Captain Keeling, but I played at billiards with him and won half a **crown** of him and the Doctor. George B-th brought home my boy Eugene. . . . In the evening I took a walk about the plantation. Eugene was whipped for running away and had the [bit] put on him. I said my prayers and had good health, good thought, and good humor, thanks be to God Almighty.

◀ **crown**
British colonial money

September 3, 1709. . . . I read some geometry. We had no court this day. My wife was **indisposed** again but not to much purpose. I ate roast chicken for dinner. In the afternoon I beat Jenny for throwing water on the couch. . . .

◀ **indisposed**
ill

Source: The Secret Diary of William Byrd of Westover, 1709–1712.

In 1539, Estevanico accompanied Spanish Friar Marcos de Niza (*NEE-zuh*) on a search for the Seven Cities of Cíbola (*SEE-bow-luh*). It was thought that these cities contained great wealth. On this journey, Native Americans, believed to be the Zuni people, killed Estevanico.

free blacks

During colonial times, some African Americans gained their freedom. There is evidence that during the 17th century some Africans came to North America as **indentured servants** (see p. 25). This

Slaves Versus Indentured Servants

The first Africans arrived in the Jamestown colony in 1619. At first, they were outnumbered by white indentured servants who had agreed to work for a master for a number of years in exchange for travel to the colony from Europe. After the term of service was over, white servants were free to leave to begin their own lives in America. As the colony grew, the number of enslaved Africans began to grow. By the start of the 18th century, there were equal numbers of white and African servants.

Year	Number of White Servants	Number of Slaves or Black Indentured Servants
1620	800	50
1650	7,200	500
1674	10,700	2,700
1686	9,500	6,000
1694	not available	9,500
1703	11,500	11,500

meant that they were freed after they fulfilled their term of service. In some cases, enslaved Africans were able to purchase their freedom from their owners. Sometimes they had their freedom purchased for them. Occasionally, a slave owner would free a slave who had served faithfully for a number of years. During the 17th and 18th centuries, as northern states ended slavery, free blacks moved north. Even freedom, however, did not bring equal rights (see **Black Codes**, p. 22).

Free black communities made up of runaway slaves also existed. These runaways were called *maroons*, a word that comes from the Spanish *cimarrones*, or runaway cattle. Maroon communities were located in heavily wooded, mountainous, or swampy areas far from population centers. These were self-sufficient communities that sometimes survived for many years.

French and Indian War

The French and Indian War (1754–1763) was a struggle between British and French forces in North America. During the war, British soldiers, colonial militia, and Native Americans fought the French and other Native Americans in Canada and on the Ohio frontier. Both free and enslaved African Americans were called to serve the British cause. In Virginia, **free blacks** (see p. 23) were called to duty in 1755; however, they were not allowed to serve in combat positions. African Americans served mainly as laborers and scouts. Whites feared that if blacks were armed, they might use their weapons to free enslaved peoples.

Germantown Protest

The Germantown Protest in 1688 was the first formal protest of the slave trade. The protest was issued by the Mennonites (*MEN-un-eyts*), a Christian group founded in the Netherlands in the 16th century. The Mennonites came to North America in the 17th century. They refused to join the military or to hold public office.

indentured servant

An indentured servant signed a contract agreeing to work for a certain number of years in exchange for passage to the Americas. Some historians believe that the first Africans who came to North America were brought as indentured servants and were freed upon fulfilling their contract.

Jamestown settlement

Jamestown was founded through a *charter* granted to the Virginia Company in 1606 by King James I. The first group of colonists arrived in 1607 and named their settlement Jamestown in honor of the king. The colony seemed doomed to failure until

Resolutions of Germantown Mennonites February 18, 1688

The Mennonites of Germantown in the colony of Pennsylvania were the first to formally protest the slave trade.

We hear that the most part of such [Negros] are brought [here to America] against their will and consent, and that many of them are stolen. Now, though they are black, we cannot conceive there is more liberty to have them slaves, as it is to have other white ones. There is a saying, that we should do to all men like as we will be done ourselves; making no difference of what generation, descent, or colour they are. And those who steal or rob men, and those who buy or purchase them, are they not all alike?

Source: *The Pennsylvania Magazine of History and Biography*, 1880

A group of enslaved Africans arrives in Jamestown Colony in 1619. They are the first known Africans in the original 13 colonies. (Library of Congress)

the colonists began planting tobacco. It was a profitable crop, but was hard to grow and required much labor. The Virginia colonists began importing enslaved Africans to work the tobacco fields. The first group arrived in 1619 on a Dutch ship. Some historians believe these first Africans were indentured servants, but later the Virginia colony passed laws making nearly all Africans enslaved.

Johnson, Anthony

Some historians believe that Anthony Johnson (ca. 1603–1670) was among the first group of 20 Africans to come to North America. This group was aboard a Dutch ship that landed in Jamestown in 1619. It is known that during the 1620s, Johnson worked on a Virginia tobacco plantation as either an indentured servant or an enslaved person. On this plantation, he met and married an African woman named Mary, and together they had four children. After a time, Anthony and Mary became free. They bought land and raised livestock. Their property soon grew to 250 acres. In 1665, the Johnsons sold 200 acres in Virginia, gave the remaining 50 acres to their son Richard, and moved to

The Anthony Johnson Case (1670)

Below is an excerpt of the verdict of the jury.

A jury of free [men] ...doth declare that the said Anthony Johnson lately deceased in his life time was seized of fifty acres of land now in the possession of Rich. Johnson in the County of Accomack aforesaid and further that the said Anthony Johnson was a negro and by consequence an alien and for that cause the said land doth **escheat** to [the British crown]. ...

◀ **escheat**
revert

Source: Library of Congress.

Maryland. Anthony died in 1670. That same year, a Virginia court began trying to deny the Johnsons' right to have owned and sold their land in Virginia. The jury decided that Johnson was "a Negro and by consequence an *alien*." Because aliens, or foreigners not considered citizens of the colony, could not own land themselves, the land was given to the British government. The decision set the stage for a future in which African Americans would be denied even more rights.

Key, Elizabeth

Elizabeth Key was the daughter of an enslaved African woman and a free white Virginian colonist. In 1636, Elizabeth became an indentured servant to a white settler for nine years, after which she was supposed to be set free. Before being released, she was sent to work for another man. When he died in 1655, Elizabeth had already been a servant for 19 years. Elizabeth and her lawyer, William Greensted, asked the court to free her based on an English law. This law stated that if a child's father was a free man, then the child should be free. The court gave Elizabeth her freedom, but the decision was *appealed* to a higher court. The high court ruled that Elizabeth was a slave. Elizabeth then *appealed* to Virginia's General Assembly. The assembly appointed a committee to investigate her case. The committee sent the case back to the courts and Elizabeth finally won her freedom. After winning the case, William Greensted married her. In 1662 Virginia passed

The Case of Elizabeth Key (1655-1656)

Elizabeth Key, the child of a white father and an enslaved African American mother, won her freedom in Virginia's colonial courts.

The first excerpt is from Elizabeth Key's first trial.

...We whose names are underwritten being impaneled upon a Jury to try a difference between Elizabeth pretended Slave to the Estate of Col. John Mottrom deceased and the overseers of the said Estate do find that the said Elizabeth ought to be free...

The excerpt below is from the General Assembly's report.

A Report of a Committee from an Assembly Concerning the Freedom of Elizabeth Key

It appears to us that she is the daughter of Thomas Key by several Evidences....That she hath bin by verdict of a Jury impaneled 20th January 1655 in the County of Northumberland found to be free by several oaths which the Jury desired might be Recorded That by the Common Law the Child of a Woman slave begott by a freeman ought to be free. That she hath been long since Christened...That Thomas Key sold her only for nine Years to Col. Higginson with several conditions to use her more Respectfully than a Common servant or slave ... For these Reasons we conceive the said Elizabeth ought to be free and that her last Master should give her Corn and Clothes and give her satisfaction for the time she hath served longer than She ought to have done.

Source: Northumberland County Record Books, 1652-1658.

a law that stated that a child's status is determined by whether the mother is free or enslaved.

Bartolomé de Las Casas. (Library of Congress)

Las Casas, Bartolomé de

Bartolomé de Las Casas (1474–1566) was born in Spain and came to Hispaniola in 1502. There he took part in fighting the Native Americans on the island. In exchange for fighting, he received a land grant, but later went to Rome and became a priest. When he returned in 1512, Las Casas was the first ordained priest in the Americas.

During this period, mistreatment of Indians by Spanish settlers was reaching its height. Las Casas fought against the abuse. He appealed to the Spanish king and queen. He called for an end

Massachusetts Body of Liberties

The Body of Liberties was the first colonial document to "legalize" slavery. At first this clause seems to indicate that slavery is illegal, but it allows slavery of those captured in war and those who "willingly sell themselves or are sold to us." It is hard to believe many people would sell themselves into slavery.

There shall never be any **bond slavery**, **villeinage**, or captivity amongst us unless it be lawful captives taken in just wars, and such strangers as willingly sell themselves or are sold to us. And these shall have all the liberties and Christian **usages** which the law of God established in Israel concerning such persons doth morally require. This exempts none from servitude who shall be judged thereto by authority.

Source: Collections, Massachusetts Historical Society.

◀ **bond slavery**
the state of being bound to service without pay

◀ **villeinage**
slavery

◀ **usages**
customs

to the poor treatment of Indians. Las Casas suggested importing Africans to the Americas to fill the labor shortage. He believed Africans were better suited for work on plantations and in mines. The Spanish monarchs agreed to allow the settlers to import enslaved Africans. This was the beginning of the transatlantic slave trade. When he saw plantation owners abusing African slaves, Las Casas began to regret his role in the slave trade. He wrote *A History of the Indies*, which was published 300 years after his death. This book expressed Las Casas's belief that all slavery was wrong.

Massachusetts Body of Liberties

The Massachusetts Body of Liberties was New England's first code of laws. It was put together by a Puritan minister and adopted by the General Court of Massachusetts in December 1641. The document listed many civil and criminal laws. It contained laws protecting the rights of men, women, and children. In spite of these protections, the document permitted the enslavement of Indians, whites, and Africans in Massachusetts.

Mather, Cotton

Cotton Mather.
(Library of Congress)

Born in Boston, Cotton Mather was a Puritan clergyman and writer. As early as 1693, Mather organized the Society of Negroes in Massachusetts. It is the earliest recorded African American religious meeting. The group met on Sunday evenings, with the permission of each enslaved person's master. They prayed, sang, and listened to sermons. Mather wrote the *Rules for the Society of the Negroes* in 1693. It contained religious teachings for the enslaved peoples to memorize. Mather told the enslaved African Americans to be loyal to their masters. He preached that they had been enslaved because they had sinned against God. Mather told enslaved African Americans that their just reward would come in heaven.

Middle Passage

The Middle Passage is the term used to describe the second, or middle, "leg" of the **triangle trade** (see p. 34) for which Africans were forced onto ships that crossed the Atlantic Ocean. Often the enslaved Africans were chained two-by-two. They were packed into the ship below deck where they had less than five feet of headroom. Since people were crushed together with little air and often no place for human waste, disease was common. Conditions on the ships were so awful that some estimate that about 20 percent of the slaves died during the passage. Many tried to kill themselves by jumping into the sea when brought on deck for fresh air and exercise. Those who refused to eat were forced to. The passage could last from 40 to 141 days, depending on weather and destination.

Pinkster Day

Pinkster Day is an African American spring festival. It got its name from a Dutch celebration. African Americans in New York's Hudson Valley region began celebrating on this day in the mid-18th century. Festivities included African dances and music, and Dutch, French, German, and Native American peoples attended the event. Today, a number of cities and towns in New York hold Pinkster Day celebrations.

Quakers

The Quakers are a Christian group that began in England in the mid-17th century. Also known as the Society of Friends, Quakers have no formal rituals or priesthood. Quakers reject violence and will not take part in war.

Selected Slave Laws

During the colonial era, the status of most Africans and African Americans moved from that of an indentured servant who could eventually earn freedom to a slave for life. Laws limited enslaved people's freedoms, created penalties for runaways, and restricted the progress of Africans in America.

from An Act for the Apprehension and Suppression of Runaways, Negroes and Slaves (Virginia, 1672)

...if any negroe, **molatto**, Indian slave, or servant for life, run away and shall be persued by the warrant or **hue and crye**, it shall and may be lawful for any person who shall endeavour to take them, upon the resistance of such negroe, molatto, Indian slave, or servant for life, to kill or wound him or them so resisting; ...

◄ **molatto**
(mulatto) a person of mixed African and white heritage

◄ **hue and crye**
public notice

from An Act Concerning Servants and Slaves (Virginia, 1705)

...no minister of the church of England, or other minister, shall hereafter wittingly presume to marry a white man with a Negro or mulatto woman; or to marry a white woman with a Negro or mulatto man, ...

if any slave resist his master, or owner, or other person, by his or her order, correcting such slave, and shall happen to be killed in such correction, it shall not be accounted felony; ...

no slave shall go armed with gun, sword, club, staff, or other weapon, nor go from off the plantation and seat of land where such slave shall be appointed to live, without a certificate of leave in writing, for so doing, from his or her master, mistress, or overseer...

all children shall be bond or free, according to the condition of their mothers...

from An Act for the Better Ordering and Governing of Negroes and Slaves (South Carolina, 1712)

...all negroes, mulatoes, mustizoes or Indians, which at any time heretofore have been sold, or now are held or taken to be, or hereafter shall be bought and sold for slaves, are hereby declared slaves; and they, and their children, are hereby made and declared slaves, to all intents and purposes; ...

Source: Library of Congress.

Slavery in the 13 English Colonies

Every one of the 13 colonies eventually legalized slavery.

Colony	Legal Recognition of Slavery
Massachusetts	1641
Connecticut	1650
Virginia	1661
Maryland	1663
New York	1665
South Carolina	1682
Pennsylvania	1700
New Jersey	1702
Rhode Island	1703
New Hampshire	1714
North Carolina	1715
Delaware	1721
Georgia	1755

In 1676, the group's founder, George Fox, said that he believed that Jesus Christ had died for Africans as well as Europeans. A number of Quakers thought the slave trade evil. These Quakers did not own slaves and spoke out against slavery. However, many Quakers did own enslaved Africans until 1758, when all Quakers stopped this practice. Many Quakers became active **abolitionists** (see page 73), sheltering runaways and helping slaves to freedom.

religion

Africans who were forced to come to the Americas generally brought with them either Islam or traditional African religions. Traditional African religions varied, depending on where they originated. Most traditional religions had in common a belief in the power of ancestral spirits, respect for the power of nature, and the belief in a Supreme Being, or God.

A number of West Africans were Muslim. When Europeans came into contact with Africans, *missionaries* tried to convert Africans to Christianity. One of the earliest efforts was the Brotherhood of the True Cross of Spaniards, founded by the Roman Catholic Church in Spain in 1540. Later, in 1701, the Church of England founded the Society for the Propagation of the Gospel in Foreign Parts. The Society offered religious instruction to African Americans and Indians. To convince reluctant slave owners to allow their enslaved peoples to attend religious instruction, the Society gave out pamphlets claiming that religion would make enslaved persons more obedient.

The Great Awakening was a religious movement in the 1730s and 1740s. During the Great Awakening, many African Americans in the English colonies were baptized. The beliefs held

Slave Revolts During the Colonial Era: A Selected Chronology

Slave uprisings struck fear in the hearts of white slave owners. Yet, slave revolts had little chance of succeeding, and participants risked harsh punishment. The fact that enslaved African Americans did rebel demonstrates their determination to win freedom.

Place	Year	Description
Hispaniola	1522	First recorded rebellion of enslaved Africans.
Mexico	1537	Enslaved Africans try to rebel, but are discovered.
Venezuela	1552	Slaves working the mines in Buria, Venezuela, revolt.
Mexico	1612	In Mexico City, 35 slaves are executed after a slave conspiracy is discovered.
New York City	1712	Twenty-five enslaved African Americans burn buildings, killing nine whites. When the rebels are caught, they are executed.
Virginia	1730	A slave conspiracy is discovered in Norfolk and Princess Anne counties, Virginia. Governor orders white males to carry arms with them, even to church.
Stono, South Carolina	1739	Led by an enslaved Angolan, a small group of enslaved Africans storms a gun shop, kills two white men, and secures weapons. More slaves join as the group tries to make its way to freedom in Spanish Florida. The rebellion ends when a colonial militia defeats the group of slaves.
New York City	1741	An alleged slave plot leads to trials, executions, and an accusation of Spanish intervention.

by the Methodist leaders of the Great Awakening included the idea that Christianity was in the heart. The Methodists allowed integrated churches and "called ministry." This meant that African Americans could preach if they had the "calling."

Royal African Company

In 1672, the English government gave a private company called Royal African Company a *monopoly* in the slave trade. The monopoly gave the company exclusive rights to buy and sell slaves in English colonies. From 1680 to 1686, the company transported

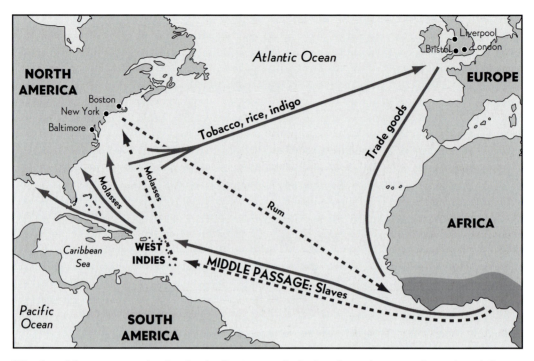

"Triangle trade" was a term used to describe the shipping route England used to exchange manufactured goods for African slaves and raw material from the Americas.

an average of 5,000 slaves a year. In 1698, Parliament opened the slave trade to all.

slave laws

Throughout the 17th and 18th centuries, laws that defined slavery in the 13 colonies became more strict. This was because owners of farms and plantations relied on the labor of enslaved African Americans. Therefore, these owners supported laws that helped them control their human "property."

slave revolts

Sometimes enslaved peoples tried to rebel against their owners. Yet, slave revolts had little chance of succeeding and those who took part risked harsh punishment. The fact that enslaved African Americans did rebel demonstrates their determination to win their freedom (see sidebar, p. 33).

triangle trade

The term "triangle trade" refers to a pattern of trade that started with the slave trade. Manufactured goods moved from British

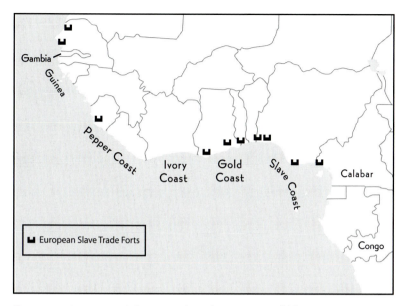

European nations operated slave ports along the west coast of Africa.

ports to the west coast of Africa. There the goods were exchanged for enslaved Africans. The enslaved peoples were shipped to the West Indies or to colonies in North or South America to work as laborers. They were exchanged for agricultural goods that were shipped back to Great Britain.

Virginia House of Burgesses

The Virginia House of Burgesses *(BUR-jes-iss)* was a lawmaking body in colonial Virginia. Throughout the 17th and 18th centuries, the House of Burgesses passed more and more harsh laws limiting the rights of both enslaved and free African Americans.

West Indies

The West Indies is an island region in the Caribbean Sea. European exploration of the region caused great hardships for the native population. They began to die of European diseases to which they had no resistance (ability to fight off). Europeans also enslaved the native population and worked them to death. During the 1500s, Spain began importing enslaved Africans to work the European-controlled sugar plantations. The region became a "point" on the triangle trade route as slave traders exported enslaved peoples and gold from Africa to the West Indies.

"Bars Fight" (1746)

Lucy Terry was an African American poet whose only surviving work is a poem titled "Bars Fight." This is the first known poem written by an African American woman. Terry came from Africa as an infant and later married a wealthy free black man named Abijah (*AH-bi-jah*) Prince, who purchased her freedom. Lucy Terry Prince was an intelligent and excellent speaker. "Bars Fight" is Terry's eyewitness account of a Native American attack on the village of Deerfield, Massachusetts, in 1746. The word "bars" means "meadow."

August 'twas the twenty-fifth,
Seventeen hundred forty-six;
The Indians did in ambush lay,
Some very valiant men to slay,
The names of whom I'll not leave out.
Samuel Allen like a hero fout,
And though he was so brave and bold,
His face no more shalt we behold

Eteazer Hawks was killed outright,
Before he had time to fight,
Before he did the Indians see,
Was shot and killed immediately.
Oliver Amsden he was slain,
Which caused his friends much grief and pain.
Simeon Amsden they found dead,
Not many rods distant from his head.
Adonijah Gillett we do hear
Did lose his life which was so dear.
John Sadler fled across the water,
And thus escaped the dreadful slaughter.
Eunice Allen see the Indians coming,
And hopes to save herself by running,
And had not her petticoats stopped her,
The awful creatures had not catched her,
Nor tommy hawked her on the head,
And left her on the ground for dead.
Young Samuel Allen, Oh lack-a-day!
Was taken and carried to Canada.

Source: Josiah Holland, *History of Western Massachusetts* (1855).

CHAPTER TWO

That All Men Are Created Equal

Slavery in Revolutionary America, 1764–1820

"As all are of one species…Liberty is Equally as pre[c]ious to a Black man as it is to a white one…a Jewel which was handed Down to man from the cabinet of heaven. …[A]n african, has Equally as good a right to his Liberty in common with Englishmen."

—Lemuel Haynes, African American minister

During the 18th and early 19th centuries, the United States struggled to become a strong, independent nation. During this era there were two wars with Britain and expansion to the west. Also during this period, both enslaved and free African Americans struggled to gain equality.

BRITAIN AND THE 13 COLONIES: TENSIONS BUILD

When the **French and Indian War** (see p. 25) ended in 1763, France gave Canada to the British, who won the war. France kept its colonies in the Caribbean. Spain, France's ally, got New Orleans, territories west of the Mississippi River, Cuba, and the Philippines.

Britain thought that its 13 American colonies would be grateful for protection against the French and those Native Americans who sided with them. However, the colonies felt used by the British. The British taxed them to help pay for the war, but would not allow them to elect officials to represent them in the British Parliament. The colonists protested with cries of "No taxation without representation." The colonists even talked of stopping the slave trade to hurt Britain's economy. However, the colonists themselves did not wish to give up the profits of the slave trade. Tension between the British and the colonists continued to grow. In 1770 a fight broke out between a group of Boston colonists and some British soldiers. The British troops killed five Americans in what became known as the **Boston Massacre** (see p. 51).

A DECLARATION OF INDEPENDENCE

Colonists who wanted a separate American nation were called Patriots. Many African Americans joined the cause of the Patriots. They thought they had a common cause. Weren't the white Americans protesting that they were "slaves" to the British? Surely they would see the connection between their situation and the enslaved African Americans. James Otis, a white political leader from Massachusetts, was one person who agreed. He spoke out defending the rights of the African Americans.

In the South, slave owners did not agree with Otis. In fact, many well-known Patriots were also slaveholders. Even Thomas Jefferson owned 200 slaves when he wrote the **Declaration of Independence** (see p. 53).

Jefferson's Declaration stated: "We hold these truths to be self-evident: that all men are created equal; that they are endowed by their Creator with certain *unalienable* rights; that among these are life, liberty and the pursuit of happiness; that to secure these rights, governments are instituted among

Timeline

1764

African Americans join the first American Methodist Society in Maryland.

1773

Jean-Baptiste Point Du Sable son of an enslaved African American mother and French father, becomes the first settler in what is now Chicago.

Thomas Jefferson, seen sitting at the left, wrote the first draft of the Declaration of Independence. A committee made up of (from Jefferson's left) Robert Livingston, Benjamin Franklin, Roger Sherman, and John Adams, helped revise it. African Americans hoped it would grant them the same freedoms as whites. (Library of Congress)

men deriving their just powers from the consent of the governed..." African Americans hoped that these ideas applied to all Americans—black and white. Jefferson and other Patriots, such as James Madison and George Mason,

1775–1781 | 1776 | 1780 | 1783

The **American Revolution** is fought. Approximately 7,000 African Americans fight in the Continental Army.

Poet **Phillis Wheatley**, an enslaved African American, meets with George Washington after writing a poem in his honor.

The religious movement known as the "Second Great Awakening" brings revival tent meetings; many of these tent meetings are interracial, as African Americans as well as whites may join.

The American Revolution ends. African Americans gain suffrage in Massachusetts mainly due to the efforts of **Paul Cuffe**.

were wealthy men who relied on slave labor to run their *estates*. They were well educated and read much about democracy and government and the natural rights of humans. However, these men refused to admit the moral and human issues of enslaving people.

AFRICAN AMERICANS AND THE AMERICAN REVOLUTION

In 1770, **Crispus Attucks** (see p. 49), a fugitive enslaved African, died in a clash with British soldiers known as the Boston Massacre. Five years later, several African Americans fought with the Massachusetts militia in early **American Revolution** (see p. 47) battles like Bunker Hill. However, when George Washington first began recruiting soldiers for the Continental Army, he was against using African American troops for fear that white men might not wish to serve alongside them. There was another problem. Since the bloody Stono rebellion in South Carolina in 1739, slaveholders were afraid to arm African men. Slave owners feared that armed African Americans would rebel and demand an end to slavery.

Virginia's Governor Dunmore offered to free any enslaved person who fought for the British. The Americans were furious. Many enslaved Africans signed up with the British army.

A fugitive slave named Colonel Tye led the British Black Brigade. At one point, it numbered 800 men. In New York, Tye's men hunted and killed Patriots and freed enslaved Africans.

1787	1789	1790	1791
Free African Society is founded in Philadelphia.	**Olaudah Equiano**, an African who was kidnapped as a child from his home in Nigeria, publishes his life story. His book gives a firsthand account of the slave trade.	Population of free African Americans reaches 59,000. The same year, the number of enslaved African Americans reaches over 697,000, and the number of white Americans reaches 1.6 million.	**Richard Allen** and **Absalom Jones** found the African Church in Philadelphia.

Before long, General Washington changed his mind about allowing African Americans to fight. During the winter of 1777 at Valley Forge, poor white soldiers had deserted Washington's army. Early in 1778, Washington accepted a Rhode Island regiment of both free and enslaved blacks. Many enslaved people took their owner's place in the army. Enslaved Africans from Massachusetts and Connecticut were promised freedom if they survived. New Hampshire offered equal pay to whites and free blacks. Eventually, 7,000 African Americans served the Patriot cause. As the war moved into the South, the British got the upper hand. They took Savannah in 1778, Augusta and Norfolk in 1779, and Charleston in 1780. As plantation owners fled, many enslaved people rode their masters' horses to join the British.

In Virginia, the Continental Army took the lead again. Washington attacked General Cornwallis at Yorktown. Because they were running out of food, the British released their African American soldiers. Many had *smallpox*. Others were starving. When Cornwallis surrendered, the Patriots found the ground covered with the bodies of African Americans. Many of the living tagged along after the British to avoid going back to being enslaved.

At the end of the war, the peace treaty said that the British would return former enslaved peoples to their owners. However, the acting British commander, Sir Guy Carleton, had second thoughts. He declared that any enslaved peoples who had joined the British before the treaty were free. If

1791	1791	1793	1794
Former slave **Toussaint L'Ouverture** leads a slave revolt against the French in Haiti.	**Benjamin Banneker**, a free black, publishes his best-selling almanac and begins an exchange of letters with Thomas Jefferson.	U.S. Congress passes The Fugitive Slave Act. Philadelphia businessman **James Forten**, an African American, is one of the signers of a petition to change the act.	South Carolina passes a law forbidding free blacks from entering the state.

this violated the treaty, Carleton said, the British would pay the former owners. Some 3,000 men, women, and children were freed right away. Nearly 20,000 left with the British military. Others left on private ships. Others were captured and sold back into slavery in the Caribbean.

SLAVERY AFTER THE AMERICAN REVOLUTION

For a while it looked as though slavery was going to end. Between 1777 and 1804, it was abolished in one way or another from Pennsylvania north. In Virginia and Maryland, some enslaved peoples purchased, or were given, their freedom. But slavery did not end.

The Revolution ruined southern crops. Labor was needed to restore the land. The wartime ban on the slave trade was lifted and the price of enslaved peoples rose again.

Even free African Americans had tough lives. In Philadelphia, African Americans were chased from the city out of fear they would take away jobs. Ohio, Maryland, Delaware, and Kentucky passed laws forbidding free African Americans from moving there. Where could they go?

Some wanted the African Americans to go back to Africa. Some African American leaders supported the movement, but most ordinary blacks resisted. In spite of the poor treatment they received, they had lived in America all their lives. They did not want to be sent away.

1800	1803	1804	1807
Gabriel Prosser's conspiracy organizes about 1,000 enslaved African Americans to march on Richmond, Virginia. The rebellion ends in failure.	The United States purchases the **Louisiana Territory** from France.	Haiti wins independence from France, becoming the second free nation in the Americas.	Britain bans slave trade in its empire.

SLAVERY UNDER THE CONSTITUTION

The new **U.S. Constitution** (see p. 62) called for a president, a two-house legislature called a Congress, and a legal system headed by a Supreme Court. To persuade slave states to cooperate, the signers extended the slave trade for 20 years. In the one house of Congress that

George Washington, like many of the United States founders, was a slave owner. (Library of Congress)

would be based on population, they agreed that men, women, and children, except Native Americans, would be counted to determine representation. Since free states worried about being outvoted by slave states, each enslaved person was counted as three-fifths of a person. No one spoke for free blacks.

THE COTTON GIN AND THE LOUISIANA PURCHASE

The possibility that slavery would slowly die out ended when Eli Whitney invented his **cotton gin** (see p. 51) in 1793. With the cotton gin, two people could clean as much cotton in one day as 100 with the usual method. In five years, the gin increased the production of cotton by 400 percent. This also increased the demand for enslaved people, since more labor was required to pick and clean the additional cotton.

1808	**1812–1815**	**1816–1843**	**1817**
U.S. Congress ends the Atlantic slave trade. The slave trade within the United States expands.	**War of 1812** takes place. African Americans play a significant role in the U.S. Navy.	**Seminole Wars** pit U.S. army against Seminole Native Americans and runaway African Americans in Florida.	**African Colonization Society** is formed by by whites to send African Americans back to Africa.

Cotton grew fast in the South. Enslaved Africans were driven to make sure that no time was lost in harvesting the profitable crop. As more planters across the South sought laborers to work their cotton fields, slave traders began to sell enslaved Africans for more and more money to meet the demand. The cotton gin helped make selling slave labor a very profitable business.

In 1803, France sold its remaining territory in North America to the United States, in what is known as the **Louisiana Purchase** (see p. 57). The Louisiana Territory stretched over 800,000 square miles from the mouth of the Mississippi River near New Orleans to the Rocky Mountains. In time, as explorers and settlers moved west into the new land, France's old Louisiana Territory would be divided up into new American states.

The first new state was Missouri. When Missouri asked to join the Union as a slave state in 1819, **abolitionists** (see p. 45) were very angry. In 1820 a compromise was reached: Missouri would be a slave state, but other states inside the Louisiana Territory would be free. It was a bargain that many would later regret.

1818	**1819**	**1820**
France and Holland end participation in the slave trade.	The United States purchases Florida from Spain for $5 million.	The **Missouri Compromise** defines free and slave states in the Louisiana Territory.

A-Z of Key People, Events, and Terms

abolitionists

Abolitionism was the movement to end slavery. Before the **American Revolution** (see p. 47), a few individuals and groups, such as the **Quakers** (see p. 30), were opposed to slavery. Abolitionist organizations sprang up and continued to grow throughout the 18th and 19th centuries. Two examples were the Pennsylvania Society for Promoting the Abolition of Slavery, founded in 1775, and the New York *Manumission* (*man-you-MISH-un*) Society, founded in 1785.

Petition by Enslaved Blacks for Freedom Presented to Massachusetts Legislature (January 13, 1777)

This petition, drafted and signed by dozens of African Americans, is an example of abolitionism during the American Revolution.

[We] have in common with all other men a natural and **inalienable** right to that freedom which the **Great Parent of the heavens** has bestowed equally on all mankind and which [we] have never forfeited by any compact or agreement whatever. ... Every principle from which America has acted in the course of their unhappy difficulties with Great Britain pleads stronger than a thousand arguments in favor of your petitioners...[that] they may be restored to the enjoyments of that which is the natural right of all men—and their children who were born in this land of liberty—not to be held as slaves.

Source: Massachusetts Historical Society.

◀ **inalienable**
that which cannot be taken away

◀ **Great Parent of the heavens**
God

At first, abolitionists said that slaveholders should be given something in exchange for freeing their enslaved peoples. Soon they were demanding the end of slavery because they believed it was morally wrong.

Abolition of slavery began in the northern states. For example, Pennsylvania's Gradual Abolition Act of 1780 offered freedom to its enslaved African Americans. By 1804 all the northern states had outlawed slavery within their borders.

African Methodist Episcopal (AME) Church

In 1787 Saint George's Methodist Episcopal Church in Philadelphia began refusing to seat African Americans on the main floor. They were forced to sit in the balconies. Among the worshippers were **Richard Allen** (see below), an African American Methodist minister, and a man named **Absalom** (*AB-suh-lom*) **Jones** (see p. 56). These two men led the African American worshippers out of the church and began to make plans for founding a church of their own.

On July 29, 1794, Allen founded the Mother Bethel African Methodist Episcopal (AME) Church on land he owned. He served as its first pastor. Soon after, AME churches were formed in a number of other cities.

While the AME churches kept most Methodist practices, the African practices of *spontaneous* hymn singing, praying, and shouting aloud marked the differences. The AME became a political and social force for African Americans. Today, the church has hundreds of branches throughout the world. (Also see **Baptist Church**, p. 49.)

Allen, Richard

Richard Allen (1760–1831) was born an enslaved person in Philadelphia and sold to the owner of a Delaware plantation in 1768. When he was 17, his master sold off most of his family. Allen turned to religion and began preaching while still enslaved. Allen purchased his freedom in 1780 and became a Methodist minister. Methodism appealed to him because of its anti-slavery stand.

As a minister, Allen began to travel with white ministers. Allen earned a reputation as a great speaker and was invited to preach at Saint George's Methodist Episcopal Church in Philadelphia.

Richard Allen.
(Library of Congress)

After experiencing racism at Saint George's, Allen and **Absalom Jones** (see p. 56) established the **Free African Society** (see p. 56). They began making plans to form an African American church. Allen also established schools for African Americans in Philadelphia, worked as an abolitionist writing pamphlets and giving sermons against slavery, and became involved in nearly every African American institution in Philadelphia. In 1794, he established the Bethel **African Methodist Episcopal Church** (see p. 46). During the **War of 1812** (see p. 62), Allen worked with Jones again to recruit over 2,000 African Americans to help protect Philadelphia from British attack.

American Revolution

When the American Revolution began in 1775, many African Americans took part (see **Crispus Attucks**, p. 49). At the battles of Lexington and Concord many enslaved and free African Americans were part of the colonial *militia*.

When the Continental Army began to organize its troops, African Americans were ready to sign on. Those in the Continental Congress were not as ready to allow them to join. Some members of Congress believed that it would be dangerous to arm African Americans—especially those who were enslaved. Southern slave owners were especially afraid that the enslaved peoples would rebel or be killed in the war. So at the start of the war, George Washington gave an order against enlisting African Americans.

Then the British army offered freedom to any African Americans who joined its troops. Nearly 20,000 African Americans enlisted with the British during the war. They believed that joining the British was their best chance to escape slavery. At the end of the war, the British freed other African Americans. They sent some to Jamaica, England, and Canada. Others were sent back to their owners or sold in the West Indies.

In 1776, the Continental Congress began to allow free African Americans to join the army. As the American army suffered heavy losses, enslaved African Americans were also permitted to join. Some enslaved African Americans served in place of their masters. Others joined because they believed in the promise of liberty and equality as stated in the Declaration of Independence.

African Americans in the American Revolution

The chart below lists only a few of the more than 7,000 free and enslaved African Americans who served in the Continental Army.

Person	Description
Caesar Tarrant	He served in Virginia's navy on the armed ship *Patriot*.
George Latchom	He saved his colonel during a British attack by dragging the colonel out of waist-high mud.
Quaco	This enslaved African American was sold by his master to the British army. He then fled to the colonial army with valuable information. In 1782, in recognition of his services, the General Assembly of Rhode Island declared Quaco a "freedman."
James Armistead	He acted as a double agent to spy on British officers. Armistead's intelligence reports helped the Continental Army win the Battle of Yorktown.
Prince Esterbrooks	An enslaved African American, he fought at Lexington in 1775 and in nearly every major battle of the American Revolution.
Peter Salem	He was an enslaved African American who fought at Lexington, Bunker Hill, and many other battles. At Bunker Hill, after British Major Pitcairne cried "The day is ours," Salem took aim and finished him.
William Flora	He fought at the Battle of the Great Bridge near Norfolk, Virginia, during the winter of 1775. He fought bravely and was commended for his service. More than 35 years later, Flora fought in the War of 1812. He brought with him the same musket he used during the American Revolution.
Agrippa Hull	A free African American, Hull served in the brigade of General John Patterson in Massachusetts. He then served General Tadeusz Kosciuszko, the Polish hero of the American Revolution.

Some African Americans fought as a part of white units and others fought in all-black units. The Black Regiment of Rhode Island was formed in 1778 and promised freedom to any enslaved person who volunteered. There was also an all-black unit from Boston, nicknamed "the Bucks of America." Another black unit, the Volunteer Chasseurs (*shass-URS*), came from French-controlled Haiti.

By the end of the war, approximately 5,000 African Americans had served in the Continental Army and 2,000 more had served in the navy. African Americans from every colony except South Carolina joined the Continental Army. African Americans had fought in nearly every major battle in the war, and they served with great honor and distinction.

After the American victory at Yorktown in 1781, African Americans who had fought in the Continental Army rejoiced. They thought that it would mean some freedom for them.

Some northern states passed laws abolishing slavery. However, the southern economy depended on slave labor. The South did not want to free these people. In 1783 Virginia passed a law that gave freedom to African American veterans, but most slave owners in the state ignored the law. Although some slave owners freed their slaves for bravery shown during the war, most did not. It would take nearly 100 years and a civil war for enslaved African Americans to win their freedom.

Attucks, Crispus

Crispus Attucks (*AT-ucks*) (1723–1770) is believed by some to be the son of an African father and a Native American mother. His last name ("attuck") means "deer" in the Natick Indian's language. Attucks lived as an enslaved person in Framingham, Massachusetts, until he escaped in 1750. On March 5, 1770, Attucks became the first person killed in the **Boston Massacre** (see p. 51), one of the conflicts leading up to the **American Revolution** (see p. 47).

Banneker, Benjamin

Benjamin Banneker was an African American who was born free in Maryland and lived all his life on his farm near Baltimore. He was educated at a small private school for whites and **free blacks** (see p. 23). As he grew into adulthood, Banneker became a farmer, astronomer, writer, mathematician, and *surveyor*.

In 1791, Banneker sent to Thomas Jefferson a copy of an almanac he had written, which became a best-seller. A year later, Jefferson recommended that Banneker join the surveying team that had begun to lay out Washington, D.C., the new U.S. capital.

Benjamin Banneker.
(Library of Congress)

Baptist Church

The first known African Baptist church in America was the Bluestone Church. It was established in 1758 on the Virginia

A Letter to Thomas Jefferson, 1791

In 1791, Banneker sent Thomas Jefferson a copy of the almanac Banneker had been compiling. In the letter that accompanied the almanac, Banneker takes issue with some of Jefferson's ideas about African Americans.

...[there] was a time when you clearly saw into the injustice of a state of slavery, and in which you had just apprehensions of the horrors of its condition. It was now that your abhorrence thereof was so excited, that you publicly held forth this true and invaluable doctrine, which is worthy to be recorded and remembered in all succeeding ages : "We hold these truths to be self-evident, that all men are created equal; that they are endowed by their Creator with certain unalienable rights, and that among these are, life, liberty, and the pursuit of happiness." Here was a time, in which your tender feelings for yourselves had engaged you thus to declare, you were then impressed with proper ideas of the great violation of liberty, and the free possession of those blessings, to which you were entitled by nature; but, Sir, how pitiable is it to reflect, that although you were so fully convinced of the benevolence of the Father of Mankind, and of his equal and impartial distribution of these rights and privileges, which he hath conferred upon them, that you should at the same time counteract his mercies, in detaining by fraud and violence so numerous a part of my brethren, under groaning captivity and cruel oppression, that you should at the same time be found guilty of that most criminal act, which you professedly detested in others, with respect to yourselves.

Source: University of Virginia.

plantation of **William Byrd** (see pp. 22). Sometime between 1773 and 1775, enslaved African Americans founded the Silver Bluff Baptist Church in Silver Bluff, South Carolina. The First African Baptist Church was established in Savannah, Georgia, in about 1788.

Throughout the 18th and 19th centuries African American communities became more and more involved with the Baptist Church. Congregations supported their own preachers who had received the "calling" to preach. In the early 1800s, Baptist churches were opened in northern cities, such as Philadelphia, New York City, and Boston. By the mid-1800s, the Baptist Church would compete with the African Methodist Episcopal Church in importance to African Americans (see also **religion**, p. 32).

A fugitive slave, Crispus Attucks, was the first to die in the Boston Massacre. (Library of Congress)

Boston Massacre

The Boston Massacre was one of the events that led to the outbreak of the **American Revolution** (see p. 47). The colonists were angry over the increasing taxes passed by Great Britain's *Parliament*. The British sent soldiers to police the protesting colonists. The residents of Boston had been forced to house and feed the soldiers. This made the colonists even more angry.

On the night of March 5, 1770, a group of colonists began taunting a group of British soldiers. The group of colonists included a *fugitive* African named **Crispus Attucks** (see p. 49). No one is sure of exactly what happened. One version is that a soldier accused of attacking a colonist raised his *musket* in self-defense. Then someone threw something at the soldier, who fired his musket. The shot hit Attucks and killed him. Then the crowd attacked the soldiers. The soldiers opened fire, and killed four more colonists.

cotton gin

Eli Whitney invented the cotton gin in 1793. This was a machine that separated the seed from the cotton fiber quickly and cheaply. Before Whitney's invention, the southern states grew mainly long-staple, seedless cotton. This type of cotton could be grown only in a small area of the South. Short-staple cotton was a hardier crop, but required separating the seed by hand.

Short-staple cotton quickly replaced tobacco as the main cash crop in the South. As the amount of farmland used to grow cotton increased, the demand for labor to pick and clean the cotton increased as well. Therefore, as the number of cotton plantations grew across the South, so did the number of enslaved Africans.

Cuffe, Paul

Paul Cuffe was a wealthy African American sea captain, shipbuilder, and merchant. Cuffe, a **Quaker** (see p. 30) who lived in New Bedford and Westport, Massachusetts, was an active member of his community. He established a school and successfully fought for the voting rights of African American taxpayers in his

Paul Cuffe.
(Library of Congress)

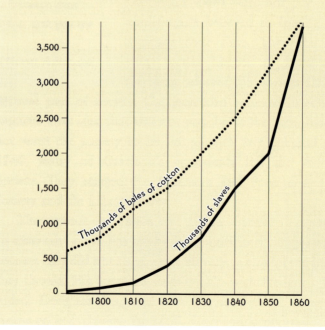

Cotton Production and Slave Labor (1800–1860)

The cotton gin made cotton "king" in the South. Since more cotton could be harvested with the cotton gin, the demand for slave labor to work those fields also increased.

The cotton gin separated the seeds from the cotton fiber. (Library of Congress)

community. In 1780, Cuffe led African American taxpayers in a protest. They complained to the state legislature about "taxation without representation," the same cry used by Patriots during the **American Revolution** (see p. 47) to protest a lack of voting rights. They demanded the right to vote, and in 1815 they received it.

In 1811, Cuffe went to Sierra Leone on the west coast of Africa. At the time, Sierra Leone was a British colony that was a safe place for former enslaved African Americans from Britain. Cuffe tried to establish a colony of African Americans in Sierra Leone. In 1815 he paid to send 38 African Americans to Sierra Leone. The project ended when Cuffe died, two years later.

Declaration of Independence

In 1776, Thomas Jefferson wrote the Declaration of Independence. The document declared the colonists' independence from Great Britain. The Declaration originally contained a passage that condemned the support for the slave trade. *Delegates* from South Carolina and Georgia objected. The economies of their states relied on slave labor. A number of northern delegates agreed. Northern ports profited from the slave trade as well. Jefferson, with help from Benjamin Franklin and others, removed the anti-slavery clause and the delegates signed the document. (See sidebar, p. 54.)

The Declaration of Independence: The Omitted Anti-Slavery Clause

Thomas Jefferson's attitude toward African Americans fluctuated during his lifetime. When he wrote the Declaration of Independence, Jefferson believed that slavery had a destructive effect on African Americans. He wrote the following clause, which was later omitted from the Declaration of Independence.

He [King George III] has waged cruel war against human nature itself, violating its most sacred rights of life and liberty in the persons of a distant people who never offended him, captivating and carrying them into slavery in another hemisphere, or to incur miserable death in their transportation thither. This **piratical** warfare, the **opprobrium of infidel powers**, is the warfare of the Christian king of Great Britain. Determined to keep open a market where MEN should be bought and sold, he has **prostituted his negative** for suppressing every legislative attempt to prohibit or restrain this **execrable** commerce.

Source: National Archives.

◄ **piratical**
like a pirate

◄ **opprobrium of infidel powers**
shameful actions usually committed by non-Christians

◄ **prostituted his negative**
misused his power to overrule colonial laws

◄ **execrable**
horrible

Du Sable, Jean-Baptiste Point

Jean-Baptiste Point Du Sable was born in 1745 on the island of Saint Domingue in the **West Indies** (see p. 35). (Saint Domingue is now divided by the nations of Haiti and the Dominican Republic). In 1773, he bought a home in Old Pioria Fort, in Illinois Territory. Five years later, he founded a trading post at the mouth of the Chicago River. Du Sable's trading post was very successful. In 1790, he built the first permanent settlement in the trading post. Although Du Sable later retired to Missouri, the trading post he founded would grow to become the nation's third largest city—Chicago, Illinois.

Equiano, Olaudah

Olaudah (oh-lah-oo-dah) Equiano (*eck-we-AHN-oh*) (ca. 1745–1797) was kidnapped from his homeland in what is now eastern Nigeria when he was about 10 years old. He was sent to the **West Indies** (see p. 35) and served a British officer and merchant. Equiano was educated and traveled widely with his master. When he was 21, he purchased his freedom and became a merchant. He was a successful businessman and became an active **abolitionist** (see p. 45). In 1787 he encouraged the British government to set up Sierra Leone as a safe place for freed enslaved persons. He also petitioned the British government to end the slave trade.

In 1789, Equiano published an autobiography describing his forced journey to the Americas and his experience as an enslaved person. The book provides a valuable firsthand account of life in Nigeria and the slave trade during the 18th century.

The Interesting Narrative of the Life of Olaudah Equiano, or Gustavus Vassa the African

In 1789, Olaudah Equiano published his autobiography. In the excerpt below, Equiano describes a slave auction.

The merchants and planters now came on board [the ship] ... They...examined us attentively. They also made us jump, and pointed to the land, signifying we were to go there.

We were not many days in the merchant's custody, before we were sold after their usual manner, which is this: On a signal given (as the beat of a drum), the buyers rush at once into the yard where the slaves are confined, and make choice of that parcel they like best. The noise and clamor with which this is attended and the eagerness visible in the countenances of the buyers, served not a little to increase the apprehension of terrified Africans...In this manner...are relations and friends separated, most of them never to see each other again. I remember, in the vessel in which I was to be brought over... there were several brothers, who, in the sale, were sold in different lots; and it was very moving on this occasion, to see and hear their cries at parting.

Source: The Schomburg Center for Research in Black Culture, New York Public Library.

Forten, James

James Forten (1766–1842) was born a **free black** (see p. 23) in Philadelphia. During the **American Revolution** (see p. 47), he served as a sailor. After the war, he earned a living as a sailmaker and eventually ran the business. He became a wealthy businessman and used his wealth to support abolition, women's rights, *temperance*, and peace. Forten supported **Richard Allen** (see p. 46) and the **AME Church** (see p. 46).

Free African Society (FAS)

Richard Allen (see p. 46), **Absalom Jones** (see below), and six other African Americans founded the Free African Society in 1787 in Philadelphia. The FAS offered a place for African Americans to worship. It was also dedicated to helping the ill, the needy, widows, and children. For this reason it was known as a mutual aid society. Eventually, other mutual aid societies sprang up in New York, Boston, and Newport, Rhode Island.

Fugitive Slave Act

The Second Congress passed the Fugitive Slave Act on February 12, 1793. It provided a way for slave owners to enforce Article IV, Section 2, of the **U. S. Constitution** (see p. 62), which declared that even if an enslaved African American escaped from a state in which slavery was legal and made his or her way to a state in which slavery was illegal, that slave would not become free. Instead, the law required that the *fugitive* be returned to his or her owner.

Jones, Absalom

Absalom Jones (1746–1818) was born an enslaved person and purchased his and his wife's freedom in 1784. He learned to read and write at a night school for African Americans in Philadelphia. He soon became a leader of the city's black community.

Jones and **Richard Allen** (see p. 46) co-founded the **Free African Society** (see above). In 1795 Jones founded the first African American church in Philadelphia. It was called the African Episcopal Church of St. Thomas. In 1804 he became the first African American Episcopal priest in the United States. During the **War of 1812** (see p. 62), Jones worked with

Fugitive Slave Act of 1793

Article 4 of the Fugitive Slave Act stated that runaway slaves were to be secured and returned to their owners. It explained that there would be punishments for those who harbored enslaved African Americans.

For the better security of the peace and friendship now entered into by the contracting parties, against all infractions of the same, by the citizens of either party, to the prejudice of the other, neither party shall proceed to the infliction of punishments on the citizens of the other, otherwise than by securing the offender, or offenders, by imprisonment, or any other competent means, till a fair and impartial trial can be had by judges or juries of both parties, as near as can be, to the laws, customs, and usages of the contracting parties, and natural justice: the mode of such trials to be hereafter fixed by the wise men of the United States, in Congress assembled, with the assistance of such deputies of the Delaware nation, as may be appointed to act in concert with them in adjusting this matter to their mutual liking. And it is further agreed between the parties aforesaid, that neither shall entertain, or give countenance to, the enemies of the other, or protect, in their respective states, criminal fugitives, servants, or slaves, but the same to apprehend and secure, and deliver to the state or states, to which such enemies, criminals, servants, or slaves, respectively belong.

Source: Library of Congress.

Richard Allen (see p. 46) to recruit over 2,000 African Americans to help protect Philadelphia from British attack.

Louisiana Purchase

In 1803, President Thomas Jefferson sent diplomats to France to purchase the city of New Orleans. The diplomats received a surprising offer. The French government offered to sell the entire Louisiana Territory. The United States purchased the Louisiana Territory for $15 million. This land stretched from the Mississippi River to the Rocky Mountains. Its purchase doubled the size of the United States. However, the territory created a problem. Some people wanted to allow slavery in the new territory and some did not. The tension between free and slave states led to a number of fierce struggles. (See **Missouri Compromise**, p. 58.)

Toussaint L'Ouverture.
(Library of Congress)

L'Ouverture, Toussaint

Toussaint L'Ouverture (*too-SANT low-vuh-CHUR*) was a leader in Haiti's fight for freedom from France. L'Ouverture (1744–1803) led more than 100,000 African enslaved people in a revolt. They eventually drove the French out. Although French emperor Napoleon Bonaparte tricked L'Ouverture into surrendering in 1803, Haiti won its independence in 1804.

Haiti's war of independence had two effects on the United States. After France's defeat, Napoleon offered to let the United States purchase the **Louisiana Territory** (see p. 57). The other result was that free and enslaved African Americans rejoiced, knowing that people of African descent had defeated slave owners and formed a new nation. This gave the African Americans new hope.

Missouri Compromise

In 1819 Missouri applied for statehood. At the time there were 11 states that permitted slavery and 11 states that had abolished slavery. The admission of Missouri as a slave state would throw the balance of power to the southern states. The South would have more votes in the Senate than would the North.

The next year, the Missouri Compromise admitted Missouri as a slave state and Maine as a free state. This kept the balance in the Senate. Another part of the agreement divided the Louisiana Territory at 36°30'N *latitude*. This was called the "Missouri Compromise Line." North of the line, slavery would never be allowed. South of the line, slavery was permitted.

Northwest Ordinance

The Congress of the Confederation passed the Northwest Ordinance in 1787. It allowed the lands north of the Ohio River and east of the Mississippi River to expand westward. It also outlined the procedure for the admission of three to five additional states. Most important, the Northwest Ordinance did not permit slavery in the Northwest Territory.

Prosser, Gabriel

Gabriel Prosser (1775–1800) lived in Virginia. He dreamed of leading African Americans to a "promised land." He believed that the land was a state that would be formed from the middle of Virginia.

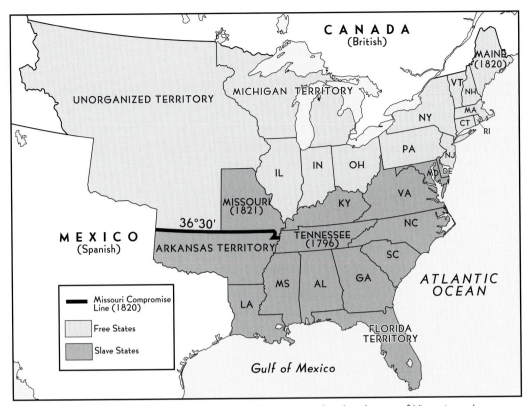

Congress passed the Missouri Compromise in 1820. Northerners agreed to the admission of Missouri as a slave state and the admission of Maine as a free state. As part of the agreement the Missouri Compromise Line was established along the latitude 36°30'N. While slavery was barred north of the line, it would be permitted south of the line.

Throughout the summer of 1800, Prosser convinced family members and other enslaved African Americans to join a revolt. On August 30, more than 1,000 enslaved people armed with axes, shovels, and any guns they could find began a march to Richmond, Virginia. They planned to put to death all whites, except Quakers, Methodists, and other groups friendly to African Americans.

As they marched, a storm struck and washed out bridges and roads. Then 600 Virginia troops arrived and the rebellion was over. Prosser tried to escape, but was caught. Prosser and more than 30 other African Americans were tried and executed.

Seminole Wars

The Seminole Native Americans lived in Florida, which was controlled by the Spanish. Georgia slave owners complained that the Seminoles were offering safety to runaway enslaved Africans. The

Northwest Ordinance Article 6

Article 6 of the Northwest Ordinance forbade slavery in the Northwest Territory. Yet it stated that fugitive slaves could not seek refuge there.

There shall be neither slavery nor involuntary servitude in the said territory, otherwise than in the punishment of crimes whereof the party shall have been duly convicted: Provided, always, That any person escaping into the same, from whom labor or service is lawfully claimed in any one of the original States, such fugitive may be lawfully reclaimed and conveyed to the person claiming his or her labor or service as aforesaid.

Source: Library of Congress.

runaways built villages and a new life near Seminole settlements. The two groups often intermarried.

In response to the slave owners' protests, the U.S. Army attacked the Seminole and African American villages in Florida. This began the Seminole Wars. In the first battle, troops led by Andrew Jackson blew up a fort where about 1,000 African American families had run. More than 300 men, women, and children were killed. Between 1816 and 1843, the United States fought three wars with the Seminoles and African Americans. During the wars, the United States took over Florida and paid Spain $5 million in 1819 for the territory. By 1843, most Seminoles—including "Black Seminoles"—had been forced to move to reservations west of the Mississippi River.

slavery

In the years during and just after the American Revolution, many northern states passed laws ending slavery. By 1804 all the states in the North either had ended slavery or had laws that set a date for the end of slavery. However, the practice of slavery was not ended for only moral reasons. It was often stopped because on small northern farms, slavery was not practical or necessary. White farmworkers and skilled craft workers complained that they could not compete for jobs with enslaved peoples.

After the Revolution, it seemed as if slavery might die out completely. Southern slave owners were finding that the costs of housing and feeding enslaved people were too great. The price of tobacco, the South's main crop, had dropped a great deal. The land was overfarmed and not fertile.

Then in 1793, Eli Whitney invented the **cotton gin** (see p. 51). Cotton became very profitable. Many field hands were required to plant and harvest cotton. Southern farmers said slavery was necessary for raising cotton.

A Slave's Epitaph: Freedom (1773)

John Jack died in Concord, Massachusetts, an enslaved African American. Many visitors have made stone rubbings of his *epitaph*, or farewell words. His grave in Concord's Hill Burying Ground can still be seen today.

GOD
Wills us free;
Man
Wills us slaves,
I will as God wills,
God's will be done.

Here lies the body of JOHN JACK,
A native of Africa, who died March, 1773,
Aged about sixty years.

Tho' born in a land of slavery,
He was born free;
Tho' he lived in a land of liberty,
He lived a slave.

Till by his honest, tho' stolen labours,
He acquired the source of slavery,
Which gave him his freedom.

Tho' not long before
Death, the grand Tyrant,
Gave him his final emancipation,
And set him on a footing with kings.

Tho' a slave to vice,
He practised those virtues,
Without which, Kings are but Slaves.

Source: Hill Burying Ground, Concord, Massachusetts.

As slavery became common in the South, African American suffering grew worse. Conditions on cotton, rice, and tobacco plantations were awful. Enslaved peoples labored from sunrise to sunset. They were given the cheapest possible housing and not enough food. When slave owners needed to sell off enslaved people, they didn't care about breaking up families. Children were sold away from mothers and husbands away from wives.

Even when allowing enslaved African Americans to convert to Christianity, slave owners were careful to tell enslaved peoples that their condition was God's will. Few enslaved African Americans believed this.

When Congress banned the Atlantic slave trade in 1808, it didn't affect enslaved African Americans very much. The slave trade in the United States remained a profitable business.

As the United States gained more territory and expanded west, slavery became a heated issue. Slave owners insisted on the right to take their human "property" to new territories and states. Abolitionists fought the spread of slavery. Debates and arguments continued until they nearly split the nation in two.

With cotton as "king," the South's economy depended on slave labor. It would take a civil war for enslaved African Americans to win their freedom.

U.S. Constitution

When delegates from the 13 states met to create a Constitution in 1787, slavery was a key issue. Delegates from the southern states wanted enslaved peoples to count as part of the population. This would give the South greater representation in Congress. The northern states argued that since enslaved peoples could not vote or pay taxes, their numbers should not be counted. After heated debate, a compromise was reached. The government would use three-fifths of the slave population for representation.

The Atlantic slave trade was another issue the delegates discussed. The delegates agreed to continue the slave trade for at least 20 years and to make enslaved peoples subject to an import tax. At the end of 20 years, Congress could vote to extend the slave trade.

The final agreement made by the delegates to the convention concerned runaway enslaved people. The delegates decided that enslaved people who escaped to "free" states did not automatically become free. Slave owners could insist upon the return of their human "property." (See **Fugitive Slave Act**, p. 56.)

War of 1812

Britain and the United States went to war again in 1812. The British had begun to arm Native Americans in the Northwest Territory to prevent westward expansion. The United States sought to put an end to British interference on U.S. territory.

Thousands of African Americans fought in the War of 1812. In Philadelphia, **Richard Allen** (see p. 46) and **Absalom Jones** (see p. 56) enlisted some 2,000 African Americans to fortify the city against British invasion. A number of African Americans fought along the western frontier and the Canadian border.

The U.S. Constitution and Slavery

At the Constitutional Convention, delegates from the states debated long and hard about the issue of slavery. In the end, several agreements were made. Below are the paragraphs of the Constitution that dealt with slavery. These paragraphs have since been stricken from the Constitution.

Article I, Section 2, Paragraph 3 (The Three-Fifths Compromise)

Representatives and direct taxes shall be apportioned among the several States which may be included within this Union, according to their respective numbers, which shall be determined by adding to the whole number of free persons, including those bound to service for a term of years, and excluding Indians not taxed, three fifths of all other persons.

Article I Section 9, Paragraph 1 (Continuing the slave trade)

The migration or importation of such persons as any of the States now existing shall think proper to admit, shall not be prohibited by the Congress prior to the year one thousand eight hundred and eight, but a tax or duty may be imposed on such importation, not exceeding ten dollars for each person.

Article IV, Section 2, Paragraph 3 (Fugitive Slave Law)

No person held to service or labor in one State under the laws thereof, escaping into another, shall, in consequence of any law or regulation therein, be discharged from such service of labor, but shall be delivered up on claim of the party to whom such service or labor may be due.

Source: National Archives.

Many African Americans joined the navy. Some estimate that about 15 percent of all seamen in the navy during the war were African American. In Lake Erie, Admiral Oliver H. Perry's force was between 10 and 25 percent African American.

From the first battles to the last one in New Orleans, African Americans contributed to the war effort. General Andrew Jackson told his African American troops, "...you surpassed my hopes. I have found in you...that noble enthusiasm which [drives one] to great deeds."

Wheatley, Phillis

At age ten, Phillis Wheatley (1753–1784) was kidnapped from West Africa and transported to Boston. She was purchased by

On Being Brought from Africa to America (1773)

By Phillis Wheatley

'Twas mercy brought me from my **Pagan** land,
Taught my **benighted** soul to understand
That there's a God, that there's a Saviour too:
Once I redemption neither sought nor knew.

Some view our **sable** race with scornful eye
"Their colour is a **diabolic** die."
Remember, Christians, Negros, black as Cain,
May be refin'd, and join th' angelic train.

Source: *The Collected Works of Phillis Wheatley.*

◀ **Pagan**
a word formerly used to describe a person who does not follow the Christian faith

◀ **benighted**
unenlightened

◀ **sable**
black

◀ **diabolic**
wicked

John Wheatley as a servant for his wife, Susannah. Phillis learned to speak English and to read and write well. Susannah never did train Phillis as a slave, but instead educated her in English, Latin, and Greek. Phillis also studied *theology* and become a devout Christian.

Phillis began writing poetry and published her first poem in 1767. At the age of 20, she published a book, *Poems on Various Subjects*, which became a great success. That same year, John Wheatley freed Phillis. She traveled to London to promote her book. Phillis met with George Washington in 1776 after writing a poem in his honor.

CHAPTER THREE

The Road to War

The Antebellum Era, 1821–1860

"America is more our country than it is the whites....The greatest riches in all America have arisen from our blood and tears...They want us for their slaves, and think nothing of murdering us...therefore... it is no more harm for you to kill a man who is trying to kill you than it is for you to take a drink of water when thirsty."

—David Walker, *Appeal to the Coloured Citizens of the World*, 1829

The **Missouri Compromise** (see p. 58) of 1820 kept a balance between slave and free states for 34 years. During those years, there was anger between those who favored slavery and those who opposed it. By the time the Missouri Compromise was ruled unconstitutional, the United States was about to break apart.

Slavery's supporters were more united than its opponents. Some, like the members of the **African Colonization Society** (see p. 73), worked to send African Americans back to Africa. Those who felt African Americans should have full citizenship in the country that they had worked so hard to build opposed them. Some supported **abolition** (see p. 73), which would be a complete end to slavery. Some simply wanted masters to free their slaves voluntarily. This was known as *manumission* (*man-you-MISH-un*). Others just wanted to stop slavery from spreading to new lands. Some who opposed the spread of slavery wanted only to protect the interests of working-class and middle-class whites. All of these different groups split from one another.

A CALL TO UNITY

African Americans had no reason to favor a gradual end to slavery. They wanted it immediately. **David Walker** (see p. 93), born a **free black** (see p. 23) in North Carolina, traveled widely, witnessing slavery's evils. In 1829, at the age of 43, he published a pamphlet. In it he urged African Americans to unite. He stressed the importance of education and **religion** (see p. 32) and respect for African heritage. Although there was a price on his head, Walker was not interested in colonization or even fleeing to Canada. When he died in 1830, many people believed he had been poisoned. No matter what the cause of death, slaveholders must have been greatly relieved.

On large plantations, the work seemed to never end. As one former field hand recalled, "The hands are required to be in the cotton fields as soon as it is light in the morning and, with the exception of ten or fifteen minutes which is given to them at noon to swallow their allowance of cold bacon, they are not permitted to be a moment idle 'til it is too dark to see, and when the moon is full, they oftentimes labor until the middle of the night…"

It is no surprise that there were revolts by enslaved people. The most successful revolt was led by **Nat Turner** (see p. 90) in 1831. Turner led attacks on a dozen white farms. He started with seven enslaved men and gathered more as he moved on. Turner's eventual band of 69 killed at least 57 over two days. Turner's men were killed, captured, or driven into hiding. In revenge, more than 120 enslaved Africans were put to death, and Turner was hanged.

Timeline

1822	1829
The Denmark **Vesey Conspiracy**, the largest attempted slave revolt in U.S. history, is discovered.	David Walker, a **free black**, publishes his *Appeal*.

There were other ways to resist. Some slaves slacked off. Others waited for the right time and slipped away. Forbidden to drum or read and write, they often communicated through codes. Religious songs, or spirituals, such as "Steal Away to Jesus" and "Wade in the Water," gave clues right under the noses of masters and overseers. Fugitives' chances for escape were improved when free people began to assist them. Over time, an informal network was formed. It was known as the **Underground Railroad** (see p. 91), and it reached from southern states all the way to Canada.

Free blacks lived better than enslaved peoples, but they were not equal to whites. Although Oberlin College permitted both blacks and whites to attend its classes, by law or custom African Americans usually could not go to school with whites, nor could they vote. Few states allowed blacks to testify in court against whites. So when white people committed crimes against African Americans, they were rarely punished. Immigrants from Ireland and Germany resented competing with free blacks for jobs in the North. In the South, most free blacks farmed. They were allowed to own property, but laws prevented anyone from freeing slaves after 1830. This made it impossible for freedmen to buy their loved ones out of slavery.

A LESSER KIND OF FREEDOM

Many people were prejudiced without cause. In the 18th century, they claimed that African Americans were lazy (even when they worked nearly

1830–1860	**1831**	**1831**	**1833**
The **Underground Railroad** helps African Americans escape from slavery.	**William Lloyd Garrison**, an abolitionist, publishes the first edition of *The Liberator*.	Enslaved African American **Nat Turner** leads a revolt.	Two **abolitionist** groups, American Anti-Slavery Society and Female Anti-Slavery Society of Philadelphia, are founded.

William Lloyd Garrison.
(Library of Congress)

around the clock seven days a week). By the mid-19th century, a form of entertainment based on this view of African Americans had become popular. Called **minstrel shows** (see p. 86), the performances featured white actors in black makeup imitating the way they thought African Americans acted.

Abolitionists argued that Africans who were allowed to learn were as smart as white people. Former slaves such as Harriet Jacobs and **Frederick Douglass** (see p. 80) offered proof that this was true. Douglass became a popular speaker and wrote his own anti-slavery journal, *The North Star*.

The white abolitionist journalist **William Lloyd Garrison** (see p. 84) was among the most radical. Garrison tried to end slavery by convincing people it was morally wrong. His newspaper, *The Liberator*, was first published in 1831, and became the most powerful abolitionist paper.

African Americans joined with white abolitionists. They refused to buy products grown by slaves. They petitioned Congress to end slavery. Some, like **Sojourner Truth** (see p. 89), also argued that African American and white women deserved the full rights of citizenship. Some people saw these as dangerous ideas. Protesters broke down the doors when the National Anti-Slavery Convention of American Women met in Philadelphia in 1838. Then they set fire to the building.

1835	**1839**	**1841**	**1841**
Oberlin College in Ohio becomes the first college that allows both blacks and whites to attend.	Enslaved Africans stage a mutiny on the *Amistad* and attempt to take the ship to Africa. The ship ends up in New York, where the Africans are arrested.	**Frederick Douglass** begins his career as an abolitionist speaker.	The Supreme Court sets free the Africans from the *Amistad*. The Africans return to Sierra Leone.

THE NATION PUSHES WEST

When Andrew Jackson, a Tennessee slaveholder, was elected president in 1828, he opened more and more farmland to white farmers. Many took enslaved African Americans to clear land in Georgia, Alabama, and Mississippi. This land had been taken from the Cherokee and other Native Americans. Jackson did not wish to kill off the Indians, but he did not want them to live among the white population. He told them they had to move further west. They could volunteer to do so, or they would be forced. In 1838, 16,000 to 17,000 Cherokee who had not volunteered to leave their homes were rounded up and set on a forced march to Oklahoma. About one-fourth of them died on a journey that became known as the "Trail of Tears." African Americans became worried over this action.

In 1841, those who opposed slavery scored one important victory. A group of Africans who had been kidnapped from Sierra Leone took over a Spanish ship, the *Amistad* (see p. 75). They sued for their freedom in Connecticut. The case was appealed to the U.S. Supreme Court, and the Africans were freed. The decision enforced the ban on international slave trading. This did not change conditions for the already enslaved—except perhaps raise their hopes in vain.

European Americans had come to think of the land all the way to the Pacific Ocean as theirs to do with as they pleased. Some even thought that God had willed it. This idea that all of America was given to the United

1843	1843	1847	1848
Sojourner Truth begins lecturing on the evils of slavery.	**Henry Highland Garnet** makes a speech at the National Negro Convention in which he calls for slaves to revolt.	Frederick Douglass founds his newpaper, the *North Star,* in Rochester, New York.	The **Free Soil Party**, an anti-slavery political party, is founded. It will later become the Republican Party.

States by God was known as "manifest destiny." After that phrase was first written about in 1845, it soon became a popular idea. It was thought the land no longer belonged to Native Americans. It certainly did not belong to people of African descent—even though some African Americans, such as mountain man **James Beckwourth** (see p. 76), had helped to explore it. Texas declared its independence from Mexico in 1836 and then legalized slavery. It was admitted to the Union in 1845. The following year, the United States went to war with Mexico and gained both California and New Mexico (which included today's Arizona, Utah, and Nevada). Abolitionists claimed it was nothing more than a war to extend slavery west.

COMPROMISE WITH A PENALTY

Those who were for slavery and those who were against it argued with each other in Congress. Each group was nervous that the other might force its position on the entire country. Three of the leading voices in the Senate on the issue were Daniel Webster of Massachusetts, Henry Clay of Kentucky, and **John C. Calhoun** (see p. 77) of South Carolina. Webster was against slavery. Calhoun believed each state had the right to decide about slavery for itself. Clay tried to find compromises between the two sides. In 1850, a new compromise was reached (see **Compromise of 1850**, p. 79). California was admitted to the Union as a free state, but a federal **Fugitive Slave Act** (see p. 56) gave slave catchers the right to track down runaways.

1849	**1850**	**1852**	**1853**
Harriet Tubman escapes from slavery in Maryland.	**Compromise of 1850** brings a strict Fugitive Slave Act and popular sovereignty.	*Uncle Tom's Cabin* by Harriet Beecher Stowe is published. The book becomes a national best-seller and turns many people angainst slavery.	Solomon Northrop's slave narrative, *Twelve Years as a Slave,* is published. Northrop, who had been a free black, had been kidnapped and sold into slavery.

Anyone who aided escaped slaves would be severely punished.

If there had been African Americans in Congress, they would never have agreed. The Fugitive Slave Act struck fear in all of slavery's enemies. Free blacks worried that they might be captured for bounty, sent into slavery, and their children kidnapped. These fears later proved to be true. Conditions for those trying to escape and their helpers on the **Underground Railroad** (see p. 91) grew more risky. Just the year before, **Harriet Tubman** (see p. 89) had escaped from a Maryland plantation. During these dangerous times, Tubman became one of the railroad's most effective *conductors*. Over time, she led about 300 people to freedom.

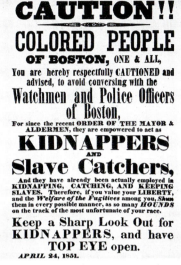

CAUTION!!
COLORED PEOPLE
OF BOSTON, ONE & ALL,
You are hereby respectfully CAUTIONED and advised, to avoid conversing with the
Watchmen and Police Officers
of Boston,
For since the recent ORDER OF THE MAYOR & ALDERMEN, they are empowered to act as
KIDNAPPERS
AND
Slave Catchers,
And they have already been actually employed in KIDNAPPING, CATCHING, AND KEEPING SLAVES. Therefore, if you value your LIBERTY, and the *Welfare of the Fugitives* among you, *Shun* them in every possible manner, as so many *HOUNDS* on the track of the most unfortunate of your race.
Keep a Sharp Look Out for
KIDNAPPERS, and have
TOP EYE open.
APRIL 24, 1851.

The Fugitive Slave Act made escape from slavery nearly impossible. (Library of Congress)

In the years leading up to the **Civil War** (see p. 108), the federal government punished African Americans even more. In 1854, the Missouri Compromise was struck down when the territories of Kansas and Nebraska were allowed to decide whether to be free or slave (see **Kansas-Nebraska Act**, p. 85). In 1857, the Supreme Court ruled against **Dred Scott** (see p. 81), a slave who had asked for his freedom on the grounds that his master had

1854	1854	1854	1857
Kansas-Nebraska Act allows residents of the territories to vote on whether or not to allow slavery in the territory.	Republican Party founded, as an anti-slavery party. Two years later, John C. Frémont runs for president as its candidate. He loses to Democrat James Buchanan.	Fugitive slave Anthony Burns is returned to his owner under the Fugitive Slave Law.	In the Dred Scott case, the U.S. Supreme Court decides that an enslaved African does not become free if his owner brings him to a free state.

taken him to a free territory. Not only was Scott denied his freedom, but the Missouri Compromise was also revoked. Although he had been one of the Supreme Court judges who had voted to free the Africans on the *Amistad* 20 years before, Chief Justice Roger B. Taney declared that African Americans "had no rights which the white man was bound to respect."

SLAVERY'S FOES UNITE

Abolitionists grew desperate. **John Brown** (see p. 76), a white radical, put together an army to attack a federal *arsenal* in Harpers Ferry, Virginia. At first in favor, Frederick Douglass became convinced that Brown's plan was reckless. He tried to talk Brown out of it, but Brown was firm. He moved ahead with an army of 17 whites and five blacks. It took the government 36 hours to put down the attack. Only three men—Brown, John Copeland, and Shields Green— survived. All were hanged.

Many people were shocked that white men would put their lives on the line against slavery, but the tide had finally turned. Within a year, **Abraham Lincoln** (see pp. 85, 119) would be elected president. Although he promised southerners not to try to end slavery, he did want to stop its spread. In the end, a war would settle the issue for good.

1859	**1860**	**1860**
John Brown leads a raid in Harpers Ferry, Virginia, hoping to begin a slave revolt.	Republican Party candidate Abraham Lincoln is elected president.	Nearly 75 percent of African American slaves work in the cotton fields.

A-Z of Key People, Events, and Terms

abolitionists

At first, abolitionists wanted to end slavery slowly. However, from the 1830s until the Civil War, they were demanding an immediate end to slavery. Abolitionists such as **William Lloyd Garrison**, (see p. 84), Arthur and Lewis Tappan, David Walker, and others wrote papers, made speeches, and organized rallies to end slavery.

The Tappan brothers, along with other abolitionists, founded the Anti-Slavery Society in New York in 1831. The Society's goal was "the entire abolition of slavery in the United States." Many whites and free African Americans supported the organization. It quickly grew powerful.

During the 1840s, a fugitive slave named **Frederick Douglass** (see p. 80) became a well-known speaker. Other fugitive and freed slaves joined Douglass in the fight against slavery.

Woman joined the movement, too. Sisters Angelina and Sarah Grimké (*GRIM-key*) were the first women to speak for the Anti-Slavery Society. Sojourner Truth was a former slave. She held the attention of many people with stories of her life as an enslaved African American. **James Forten's** (see p. 56) three daughters, Margaretta, Harriet, and Sarah, were active abolitionists. They started the Philadelphia Female Anti-Slavery Society in 1833.

As slavery spread west into new territories, the arguments over slavery grew. During the 1840s and 1850s, new political parties were formed based on abolition. These were the Liberal Party, the **Free Soil Party** (see p. 82), and the **Republican Party** (see p. 87). As the North and South argued over slavery, the nation moved closer to war.

African Colonization Society (ACS)

In 1817 Reverend Robert Finley began the African Colonization Society (ACS). Its goal was to help free blacks immigrate to

African Americans React to the African Colonization Society

A few weeks after the African Colonization Society was founded, Philadelphia's African American community met. Thousands attended the meeting in Richard Allen's Bethel Church. It became clear that most African Americans did not support colonization. The statement below reflects their feelings.

Whereas our ancestors (not of choice) were the first cultivators of the wilds of America, we their descendants feel ourselves entitled to participate in the blessings of her luxuriant soil, which their **blood and sweat manured**; and that any measure, or system of measures, having a tendency to banish us from her bosom, would not only be cruel, but in direct violation of those principles, which have been the boast of the republic.

[It is resolved] That we never will separate ourselves voluntarily from the slave population in this country; they are our brethren by the ties of **consanguinity**, of suffering, and of wrongs; and we feel that there is more virtue in suffering privations with them, than fancied advantages for a season.

Source: Library of Congress.

◀ **blood and sweat manured**
hard work helped make grow and prosper

◀ **consanguinity**
blood

Africa. People had different reasons for supporting or attacking the organization. Many slaveholders supported the ACS. They wanted to be rid of African Americans who wanted to end slavery. Some ACS members believed that the only way African Americans would live a free life was to go to Africa. Also, some whites just wanted all African Americans to leave the United States. They were simply racist.

A number of important African American leaders, such as **Paul Cuffe** (see p. 52), **James Forten** (see p. 56), and **Richard Allen** (see p. 46), supported colonization but not the ACS. They were afraid that the ACS would force free African Americans to immigrate to Africa. Most African Americans were not interested in colonization. They had been born in the United States and thought of it as their home. Many free African Americans did not want to leave the United States while most blacks were still enslaved.

The ACS had powerful political supporters. Congressmen Henry Clay and John C. Calhoun were members. The organization's first president was Bushrod Washington, George Washington's nephew. During the 19th century the organization's popularity grew. In 1822, the ACS sent about 13,000 African Americans to Liberia. The ACS continued to work toward its goal until after the Civil War.

After the war, the goals of the ACS changed from colonization to education and the spread of Christianity in Liberia. The ACS finally broke up in 1964.

Amistad Case

In February 1839, Portuguese slave traders sailed to Sierra Leone in West Africa. They kidnapped 53 Africans and sold them as slaves to two Spanish men. They all set sail for the Caribbean on a ship named the *Amistad*. The Africans took over the ship and killed the captain and cook. Then the

A Letter from Ka-le to John Quincy Adams

Ka-le was one of the captured Africans from the *Amistad* and one of the first who learned English. His letter to Adams presents the point of view of the captured Africans.

Dear Friend Mr. Adams,

I want to write a letter to you because you talk to the grand court. . . . We want you to ask the court what we have done wrong. . . . What for Americans keep us in prison? . . . Some people say Mendi people crazy; Mendi people **dolt**, because we no talk American language. Merica people talk no Mendi language; Merica people dolt? . . . Mendi people think, think, think. All we want is make us free.

Source: Massachusetts Historical Society.

◀ **dolt**
stupid

Africans ordered the crew to sail east back to Africa. For two months, the crew sailed slowly east during the day, but at night secretly turned the ship back west. The ship ran out of supplies and some of the Africans died of starvation. The *Amistad* reached New York and was held by the U.S. Navy. The Spaniards demanded the return of their property—the Africans they had purchased. The U.S. court, however, jailed the Africans on charges of murder.

The charges of murder were dropped. The court decided that since the Africans had been kidnapped, they had a right to use force to escape. Still, the Africans were held on other charges. **Abolitionists** (see p. 73) took up the cause of the Africans. They argued that since the slave trade had been banned, the Africans had been captured illegally. Former President John Quincy Adams defended the Africans. In 1841, the Supreme Court freed the Africans. The 35 remaining Africans returned to Sierra Leone. The rest had either died at sea or while in prison.

Beckwourth, James Pierson

James Beckwourth. (Library of Congress)

An African American, James Beckwourth (1798–1866) spent most of his life exploring the western frontier. He was one of the first Mountain Men. These were people who knew how to survive in the wilderness. They made a living hunting and trapping fur-bearing animals.

Beckwourth moved west and became a fur trapper. He traveled much of North America from Florida to the Pacific Ocean and from southern Canada to northern Mexico. In the Sierra Nevada Mountains he found a mountain pass. The Beckwourth Pass allowed settlers to move through the mountain range into California.

Brown, John

John Brown. (Library of Congress)

John Brown was born in 1800 in Connecticut, but grew up in Ohio. He thought it was necessary to take strong action against the evils of slavery. During one speech, Brown shouted, "Talk! Talk! Talk! That will never free the slaves. What is needed is action!" Brown joined the **Underground Railroad** (see p. 91) and assisted hundreds of African Americans fleeing from slavery.

Then he moved to Kansas after the passage of the **Kansas-Nebraska Act** (see p. 85) in 1854. There was so much violence between those who were for and against slavery that newspapers called the Kansas territory "Bleeding Kansas." Brown led a raid on pro-slavery settlers in Pottawatomie (*poh-tuh-WOT-uh-me*) Creek. They dragged five settlers from their beds and murdered them.

Brown decided that even more extreme action was needed. On the night of October 16, 1859, Brown led 18 men into Harpers Ferry, Virginia. The group took control of a warehouse full of weapons. They gave the weapons to enslaved African Americans. They were planning a revolt, but it didn't happen. Brown and his followers were arrested and put on trial for treason. John Brown was sentenced to death by hanging.

Brown became a hero to **abolitionists** (see p. 73) and enslaved African Americans. Southerners were very angry that some abolitionists praised Brown's actions. Brown's raid at Harpers Ferry led to more division between northerners and southerners.

Burns, Anthony

Anthony Burns was an enslaved African American from Virginia. In 1854, Burns hid aboard a ship that was sailing to Boston. But his master found him, and according the **Fugitive Slave Act** (see p. 56) of 1850 he had to be returned to his master. **Abolitionists** (see p. 73) held a protest. Led by a white minister, a crowd stormed the courthouse. They tried to free Burns. In the clash, a deputy marshal fell dead. Federal troops came to restore order. Then President Franklin Pierce sent a telegram to the local district attorney. It said to "insure execution of the law." In the trial that followed, Burns lost his freedom. Even an attempt by abolitionists to purchase Burns's freedom was denied.

Anthony Burns.
(Library of Congress)

Burns was returned to Virginia on a U.S. gunboat. About 1,500 soldiers marched him to the ship. An estimated 50,000 abolitionists lined the streets in protest. Buildings were draped in black as if in mourning. Burns's trial was an example of the extremes to which abolitionists and pro-slavery forces were willing to go.

Calhoun, John C.

John Caldwell Calhoun (1782–1850) was a leading 19th-century politician. He served as South Carolina's senator, as secretary of war,

The Anthony Burns Case

In 1854, Anthony Burns escaped from slavery. From Virginia, he fled to Boston, but was soon found by his master. The trial of Anthony Burns gained national attention and tested the strength of the Fugitive Slave Law. The court found Burns guilty, and he was returned to his master. The following is an excerpt from a letter Burns wrote while in jail.

When I was going home one night I heard some one running behind me; presently a hand was put on my shoulder, and somebody said: "Stop, stop; you are the fellow who broke into a silversmith's shop the other night." I assured the man that it was a mistake, but almost before I could speak, I was lifted from off my feet by six or seven others, and it was no use to resist. In the Court House I waited some time, and as the silversmith did not come, I told them I wanted to go home for supper. A man then come to the door; he didn't open it like an honest man would, but kind of slowly opened it, and looked in. He said, "How do you do, Mr. Burns?" and I called him as we do in Virginia, "master!"

He asked me if there would be any trouble in taking me back to Virginia, and I was brought right to a stand, and didn't know what to say. He wanted to know if I remembered the money that he used to give me, and I said, "Yes, I do recollect that you used to give me twelve and a half cents at the end of every year I worked for you." He went out and came back next morning. I got no supper nor sleep that night. The next morning they told me that my master said that he had the right to me, and as I had called him "master," having the fear of God before my eyes, I could not go from it. Next morning I was taken down, with the bracelets on my wrists—not such as you wear, ladies, of gold and silver—but iron and steel, that wore into the bone.

Source: Library of Congress.

secretary of state, and vice president. Calhoun was a pro-slavery politician. He worked to protect the interests of slaveholders.

Before the Civil War, Calhoun, along with Henry Clay and Daniel Webster, led the debate over slavery. A main point of debate was whether slavery would be allowed in the western states. In 1850, Calhoun argued that slavery must be allowed in the states. He also argued that fugitive enslaved people must be returned to their owners. Calhoun stated that if the South did not get what it asked, "let the states . . . agree to separate and part in peace." The **Compromise of 1850** (see p. 79) kept the states from splitting apart at that time. Before the Compromise was passed, Calhoun died.

Coffin, Levi

Levi Coffin (1789–1877) was a Quaker and a key member of the **Underground Railroad** (see p. 91). Over a 20-year period, Coffin and his wife, Catherine, helped over 3,000 enslaved Africans escape. The Coffin home in Indiana was one of the safest "stations" on the Underground Railroad. All of the enslaved people who passed through the house made it to freedom.

Compromise of 1850

After the Mexican War (1846–1848), the United States gained a large territory in the West. There was huge debate over whether the new states formed there would allow slavery or be free. The decisions made by Congress resulted in the Compromise of 1850. The agreement had four main parts:

1. California was admitted as a free state.

2. The rest of the territory won in the war would be divided into the New Mexico and Utah territories. Citizens in each state would vote on whether or not they wanted slavery. It was an idea called popular *sovereignty* (*SAHV-ren-tee*).

3. The slave trade in Washington, D.C., would be stopped. However, it was decided that Congress had no right to stop the slave trade between slave states.

4. The **Fugitive Slave Act** (see p. 56) of 1850 was passed.

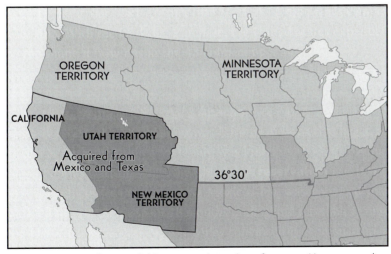

In the Compromise of 1850, California was admitted as a free state. However, popular sovereignty, or a majority vote by white citizens in each territory, would determine if slavery would be legal in other territories.

The Meaning of July Fourth for the Negro (1852)

On July 5, 1852, Frederick Douglass spoke at a gathering to celebrate the signing of the Declaration of Independence in Rochester, New York. There, he gave a speech that has become one of his most famous. It was a biting attack on slavery and the meaning of freedom.

What, to the American slave, is your 4th of July? I answer; a day that reveals to him, more than all other days in the year, the gross injustice and cruelty to which he is the constant victim. To him, your celebration is a **sham**; your boasted liberty, an unholy license; your national greatness, swelling vanity; your sounds of rejoicing are empty and heartless; your **denunciation** of tyrants, brass fronted impudence; your shouts of liberty and equality, hollow mockery; your prayers and hymns, your sermons and thanksgivings, with all your religious parade and solemnity, are, to Him, mere **bombast**, fraud, deception, **impiety**, and hypocrisy—a thin veil to cover up crimes which would disgrace a nation of savages. There is not a nation on the earth guilty of practices more shocking and bloody than are the people of the United States, at this very hour.

Source: *The Life and Writings of Frederick Douglass*, Volume 2.

◀ **sham**
fraud or deception

◀ **denunciation**
criticism

◀ **bombast**
self-importance, boasting

◀ **impiety**
sin or wickedness

Frederick Douglass.
(Library of Congress)

Douglass, Frederick

Frederick Douglass was born an enslaved person in Maryland in 1818. His given name was Frederick Augustus Washington Bailey. His early years were spent on a plantation. When he was about eight years old, Frederick was taken to live with a carpenter in Baltimore. There he learned to read and write. He also learned of the **abolitionist** (see p. 73) movement.

At the age of 15, Frederick was sent to a plantation run by Edward Covey. Covey was a cruel man, one known as a "slave-breaker." Frederick was whipped and beaten daily. In 1836, he decided to run away, but his plan was discovered and he was jailed. Two years later, he did escape to New Bedford,

Massachusetts. He married a free African American woman. The couple took the name Douglass.

In Massachusetts, Douglass became involved in the abolitionist movement and met **William Lloyd Garrison** (see p. 84). Guided by Garrison, Douglass became one of the best-known abolitionists of his day. His speeches about his life as an enslaved person were powerful and moving.

In 1845, Douglass published his autobiography, *Narrative of the Life of Frederick Douglass, an American Slave.* In 1848 he began to publish a four-page weekly paper, the *North Star.* Douglass also gave many anti-slavery speeches in Europe and the United States.

During the 1850s, Douglass and Garrison disagreed. Garrison's views were much more radical than Douglass's. They did not come back together until after the Civil War. During the war, Douglass met with **Abraham Lincoln** (see pp. 85, 119). Douglass got northern African Americans to join the Union Army. After the war Douglass fought for the rights of women as well as African Americans. He died in 1895.

Dred Scott Case

Dred Scott was an enslaved African American whose master brought him from Missouri, a slave state, to Illinois, a free state, in 1833. Scott sued for his freedom in 1846. Scott and his lawyers argued that when he entered free territory, he became free.

After making its way through the lower courts, Scott's case reached the U.S. Supreme Court in 1857. Chief Justice Roger B. Taney was charged with delivering the Court's decision.

Scott's case was based on three issues. Was Scott a citizen and therefore allowed to use the justice system to sue for freedom? Did his residence in a free state grant him freedom? Was the Missouri Compromise constitutional? The Court ruled that African Americans, free or enslaved, were not U.S. citizens. Taney said that the freedoms contained in the Declaration of Independence and the U.S. Constitution did not apply to African Americans. This meant that Scott did not even have the right to sue in court. Also, Scott was not entitled to freedom in a free state. The Court decided that as an enslaved person, Scott was

Dred Scott.
(Library of Congress)

the property of his master. The Court had no right to tell someone where he or she could take his or her property. Finally, the Missouri Compromise was ruled unconstitutional. The Court said that the law could not tell people what to do with their property.

The Court's ruling in the Dred Scott case angered northerners and delighted southerners. The Court seemed to confirm the southern belief that enslaved peoples were merely property without rights. A few others saw the possibility of hope for a quick end to slavery in the Court's ruling. **Frederick Douglass** (see p. 80) thought that the ruling would create even more opposition to slavery and would perhaps end slavery faster than expected.

Free Soil Party

The Free Soil Party was an anti-slavery political party. Its members were against allowing slavery in the new western states. Anti-slavery Democrats and Whigs began the party in 1848. They wanted to break away from the Democratic Party, which seemed to be controlled by southern slaveholders.

In 1848, the Free Soil Party combined their efforts with other anti-slavery parties and other Democrats. They nominated former President Martin Van Buren to run again. In the election, the party won 10 percent of the popular vote, and did not win any states. Zachary Taylor, the Whig candidate, became president. Taylor was a slaveholder. The Free Soil Party did elect 13 of its candidates to Congress. This was an amazing feat for a new political party.

In 1854, Free Soilers, northern Democrats, and anti-slavery Whigs formed a new party. It was called the Republican Party.

Fugitive Slave Act of 1850

The Fugitive Slave Act of 1850 was passed as part of the Missouri Compromise. It forced the return of runaway slaves and put harsh penalties on those who helped them. If convicted of allowing a runaway to escape, a person would pay a $1,000 fine and spend six months in jail. The law outraged **abolitionists** (see p. 73) and increased tensions between the North and the South.

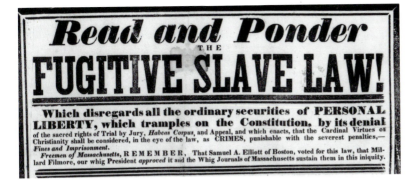

William Lloyd Garrison's newspaper attacked the Fugitive Slave Act of 1850.
(Library of Congress)

Garnet, Henry Highland

Born an enslaved person in 1815, Henry Highland Garnet became a fugitive at a young age. He ran to New York City and was educated at the African Free School. Garnet then went to the Oneida Institute in New York and became a minister.

Garnet was one of the leading **abolitionists** (see p. 73) and an inspiring speaker. Early in his career, he believed that the abolition of slavery would come about through peaceful political means. Then, in 1843, Garnet had a change of heart. He decided that radical action was needed and that a slave revolt was necessary to end slavery. At the National Negro Convention in 1843, Garnet gave a speech in which he told enslaved African Americans to rise up and rebel against their masters.

Frederick Douglass (see p. 80) and a number of other abolitionists disagreed with Garnet. At this time, most abolitionists favored a nonviolent approach. The delegates to the convention voted on whether or not to make Garnet's "Call to Rebellion" part of the convention's official platform. By just one vote, they decided not to accept Garnet's position.

Several years later, Garnet supported immigration to Africa. During the early 1850s, he traveled to Europe and lectured in England and Scotland. In 1852, he moved to Jamaica to do missionary work. Eventually, he returned to the United States.

Most abolitionists never came to accept Garnet's radical ideas about rebellion and emigration. He began to focus on his work as a minister, and during and after the Civil War was active in improving the condition of newly freed African Americans. The

A Call to Rebellion (1843)

Henry Highland Garnet's speech at the 1843 National Negro Convention surprised many of those attending. Garnet called for a massive slave rebellion to put an end to slavery. This was a radical departure from most of the convention's attendees. Below is an excerpt from the speech.

Brethren, arise, arise! Strike for your lives and liberties. Now is the day and the hour. Let every slave throughout the land do this, and the days of slavery are numbered. You cannot be more oppressed than you have been—you cannot suffer greater cruelties than you have already. Rather die freemen than live to be slaves. Remember that you are FOUR MILLIONS!

Source: Rev. Henry Highland Garnet, *A Memorial Discourse*.

U.S. government appointed Garnet as its representative in Liberia, West Africa, in 1881, but he died two months after his arrival there.

Garrison, William Lloyd

William Lloyd Garrison (1805–1879) became an **abolitionist** (see p. 73) in his twenties. He joined the **African Colonization Society** (see p. 73). He left after he realized that most members were not interested in the abolition of slavery.

From 1831 until 1865, Garrison published an antislavery newspaper called *The Liberator*. It called for an immediate end to slavery.

In 1833, Garrison and a group of fellow abolitionists started the American Anti-Slavery Society. The group fought for an end to slavery and for the rights of African Americans. However, some of Garrison's views were not popular. Most abolitionists believed in freeing enslaved Africans over time. They didn't know what would happen to freed Africans. Garrison believed that former slaves could become part of society. Garrison also believed in equality for women. That idea that was not popular at the time. Also, he did not want the society to be linked with any political party. In 1840, many of Garrison's opponents left the Anti-Slavery Society. They started the American and Foreign Anti-Slavery Society and the Liberty Party.

Throughout the 1840s and 1850s, Garrison's reputation as an extremist grew. For example, he criticized *clergy* of all faiths because they did not stand up to slavery as strongly as he thought they should. His longtime relationship with Frederick Douglass ended. Douglass disagreed with Garrison about using political means to end slavery. In 1860, Garrison supported **Abraham**

Lincoln (see below and p. 119) for president. After the 13th Amendment abolished slavery, Garrison resigned from the American Anti-Slavery Society.

Kansas-Nebraska Act

The Nebraska Territory was north of the latitude 36°30'N. According to the Missouri Compromise, the territory was "free." In 1854, Illinois Senator Stephen Douglas introduced a bill to organize the Nebraska Territory. His aim was to build a railroad that would benefit his state. However, southerners objected to his plan.

The Kansas-Nebraska Act split the Nebraska Territory into two territories: Kansas and Nebraska. It also *repealed* the Missouri Compromise. It stated that slavery would be decided in the territories by "popular sovereignty." This meant the citizens of a territory would vote to decide whether slavery would be allowed. Douglas thought non-slaveholders would live in the northern territories. The soil was not suited to cotton or other "plantation" crops. Douglas did not expect the trouble that would come between the pro- and anti-slavery settlers in the region.

Lincoln, Abraham

Abraham Lincoln (1809–1865) was the 16th president of the United States. Lincoln grew up poor and moved with his family from Kentucky to Indiana when he was seven years old. Highly intelligent, Lincoln read books and practiced writing on his own. As a grown man, Lincoln moved to Illinois and became a lawyer. He served four terms in the state legislature and one term in Congress.

In 1858, Lincoln ran for the Senate against Stephen Douglas. The two held a series of debates. They tried to portray each other as *extremists* (*eks-TREEM-ists*). Lincoln was accused of being an **abolitionist** (see p. 73). The truth was that he was only against slavery spreading into the territories west of the Mississippi. He did not oppose slavery in the states where it already existed. Douglas was portrayed by Lincoln as pro-slavery, which Douglas was not. In a famous speech, Lincoln described the nation as a house divided by slavery and stated, "A house divided against

Abraham Lincoln.
(Library of Congress)

itself cannot stand." Douglas said that slave and free states could exist together. Although Douglas won the election to the Senate, Lincoln gained national recognition.

In 1860, Lincoln was the Republican Party's presidential nominee. He won the election and the South panicked. They believed that Lincoln's speeches, such as the "House Divided" speech, proved that he planned to abolish slavery. The southern states seceded from the Union in 1861, forming the Confederate States of America. This began the Civil War. During the war, Lincoln's steady leadership helped bring victory to the Union. In 1863, in the midst of war, Lincoln issued the **Emancipation** (*ee-mans-ih-PAYSH-un*) **Proclamation** (see p. 113), a document that freed the enslaved Africans in the states that had left the Union.

In 1864, Lincoln was elected president again. Just six months after the election, the South surrendered and the Civil War was over. Just one week after the end of the war, John Wilkes Booth assassinated Abraham Lincoln. Booth was a southern actor who supported the Confederacy. The nation mourned the loss of a great leader. (Also see **Abraham Lincoln**, p. 119.)

minstrel shows

The minstrel show was a form of entertainment that began in the 1840s. White performers would put on "blackface." They would imitate what they perceived to be the speech patterns of African Americans. Full of racist and insulting remarks, minstrel shows portrayed African Americans as unintelligent fools. In spite of the insults, the shows were very popular with white audiences in both the North and the South.

Northup, Solomon

During the 1800s, even free African Americans could be caught by slave catchers. Solomon Northup was one such man. He was a free African American from New York. Northup was visiting Washington, D.C., in 1845, when slave traders captured him. They took him to New Orleans. For 12 years Northup labored in the cotton fields with other enslaved peoples. He experienced the terrible conditions under which enslaved people labored. When friends finally freed him in 1858, Northup wrote a book, *Twelve Years a Slave*, about the slave experience.

Twelve Years a Slave, Narrative of Solomon Northup (1858)

Solomon Northup was a free African American who was kidnapped and sold into slavery. When he was freed, he wrote about his experiences. Below is his description of bringing in the cotton.

The day's work over in the field, the baskets are "toted," or in other words, carried to the gin-house, where the cotton is weighed. No matter how fatigued and weary he may be—no matter how much he longs for sleep and rest—a slave never approaches the gin-house with his basket of cotton but with fear. If it falls short in weight—if he has not performed the full task appointed him, he knows that he must suffer. And if he has exceeded it by ten or twenty pounds, in all probability his master will measure the next day's task accordingly. So, whether he has too little or too much, his approach to the gin-house is always with fear and trembling. Most frequently they have too little, and therefore it is they are not anxious to leave the field. After weighing follow the whippings; and then the baskets are carried to the cotton house, and their contents stored away like hay, all hands being sent in to tramp it down.

Source: Solomon Northup, *Twelve Years a Slave.*

Republican Party

The Republican Party was founded by members of the **Free Soil Party** (see p. 82) and anti-slavery Whigs and Democrats. In 1856, the party nominated its first candidate. Presidential candidate John C. Frémont carried 11 of 16 northern states. Although he won none of the 15 southern slave states, the election proved the Republican Party to be the strongest political party in the North. In 1860, the party nominated **Abraham Lincoln** (see pp. 85, 119) for president. Lincoln won, and as he took office, the South broke away from the Union.

slave narratives

Slave *narratives* are the published stories of enslaved African Americans. They showed slavery from the enslaved people's point of view. They told of the humiliation, inhumane punishments, and harsh labor. The narratives also told of a slave culture that tried to rise above the hardships of daily life. They described the

Selected Slave Narratives

A number of slave narratives were published in the years before the Civil War. They testified to the cruelties of slavery. Below is a list of several well-known authors and the titles of their books. Most are still available either at the library or online.

Author	Narrative
Frederick Douglass	Narrative of the Life of Frederick Douglass (1845)
William Wells Brown	Narrative (1849)
Solomon Northup	Twelve Years a Slave (1858)
Harriet Jacobs	Incidents in the Life of a Slave Girl (1858)
Charles Ball	Fifty Years in Chains; or, the Life of an American Slave (1858)
James W. C. Pennington	The Fugitive Blacksmith or, Events in the History of James W. C. Pennington (1849)
Henry Bibb	The Narrative of the Life and Adventure of Henry Bibb, an American Slave (1849)

importance of family and African traditions and how they blended with American culture.

Some freed enslaved people, such as **Frederick Douglass** (see p. 80) and **Solomon Northup** (see p. 86), wrote their own narratives. Many could not read or write, so they dictated their stories to **abolitionists** (see p. 73). Many slave owners tried to say the stories weren't true.

slavery

Slavery on southern plantations in 19th-century America was brutal. Enslaved people worked from sunrise to sunset. Any northern free black or enslaved African working on a small farm or as a laborer in a small southern village, town, or city feared being sold "down river" to these types of plantations of the Deep South.

Large plantations had overseers to supervise the work. Black slave drivers aided the overseers. If the enslaved people did not work hard enough or fast enough, they could be whipped. After laboring into the night, they still had to take care of the animals and chop firewood. After all the work was done, enslaved Africans ate their small portions of food and slept until just before daybreak.

There were enslaved African Americans who were house servants, cooks, tailors, and craft workers. These people worked in conditions that were better than those in the fields. However, they were often abused and beaten by their owners.

Sojourner Truth.
(Library of Congress)

Truth, Sojourner

Isabella Baumfree (ca. 1797–1883) was born into slavery in upstate New York. She worked for a number of masters until 1827, when she was freed.

Isabella Baumfree changed her name after she had a religious experience. It convinced her that her true calling was to actively join the fight against slavery. Baumfree took the name Sojourner Truth and began preaching against slavery throughout the North and Midwest. She also spoke out in favor of women's rights.

Tubman, Harriet

Harriet Tubman (ca. 1820–1913) was born an enslaved person in Maryland. She was beaten by her owner and his workers from the time she was seven years old. She resolved from then on to fight against injustice. When she was 13, she tried to save another enslaved person from being beaten. Her owner hit her on the head with a stone. She suffered a fractured skull, an injury that affected her entire life.

In 1849, Tubman learned that she was to be sold into the Deep South. To an enslaved person, this meant a life of misery. That night Tubman ran away. She later recalled that she had only one thought: she would have either freedom or death. Tubman was lucky enough to reach the North alive.

"Ain't I a Woman?"

According to Frances Dana Gage, the organizer of an 1851 women's rights convention in Ohio, Sojourner Truth, an African American abolitionist, spoke these words to a crowd at that convention. Truth believed in equality for all, and as such worked for both women's rights and abolition.

I have ploughed and planted and gathered [crops] into barns, and no man could head [do better than] me! And ain't I a woman? ... I have borne thirteen children and seen them most all sold off to slavery .... And ain't I a woman?

Source: *New York Independent*, April 23, 1863.

Harriet Tubman.
(Library of Congress)

Tubman settled in Philadelphia. Although she was now free, she could not forget the family and friends she had left behind. She met with **abolitionists** (see p. 73) and became one of the chief *conductors* on the **Underground Railroad** (see p. 91). Tubman made a total of 19 trips to save more than 300 others from a lifetime of enslavement. She became so well known that slave owners put a price of $40,000 on her head. No one was able to collect the prize—Tubman outsmarted all the slave catchers.

Turner, Nat

Nat Turner (1800–1831) was an enslaved person from Virginia. From a young age, Turner felt that he was being prepared for a special purpose. In February 1831, Turner thought an eclipse of the sun was a sign from God. In August, Turner and eight other African Americans set out on a mission. They murdered Turner's master and everyone in his house. Turner's group then set out for the next plantation. Along the way, they picked up about 60 supporters. The group killed at least 57 whites.

A *militia* began searching for Turner and his group, but Turner managed to escape. People panicked and put dozens of innocent African Americans to death. Turner was able to remain in hiding until the end of October. On November 5, 1831, a judge sentenced Turner to death.

Turner became a martyr to African Americans all over the South. Enslaved persons told stories of "Old Nat's war." But to southerners Nat Turner was not a hero. Southern legislators passed even stricter slave laws.

Uncle Tom's Cabin

Uncle Tom's Cabin, a novel by Harriet Beecher Stowe, was published in 1852. It told of an enslaved family that suffered under a cruel *overseer*. *Uncle Tom's Cabin*

Confessions of Nat Turner (1831)

An enslaved African American from Virginia, Nat Turner believed that God was preparing him for a special mission. In 1825, the message came. Here is how Turner described it.

White spirits and black spirits engaged in battle, and the sun was darkened—the thunder rolled in the Heavens, and blood flowed in streams— and I heard a voice saying, "Such is your luck, such you are called to see, and let it come rough or smooth, you must surely bare it."

Source: Library of Congress.

Harriet Beecher Stowe's *Uncle Tom's Cabin* was such a popular book that it was also produced as a play. This poster advertises a performance of the play. (Library of Congress)

convinced many Americans to support the anti-slavery move-ment. The novel was turned into a very popular play that was performed all over the North.

Underground Railroad

The Underground Railroad (see map, p. 92, and sidebar, p. 93) was a network of escape routes that slaves took to leave the South. It operated from about 1830 to 1860. Among its most important figures were **Harriet Tubman** (see p. 89) and **Levi Coffin** (see p. 79). Along the "railroad" were "stations," or safe houses, often in the homes of sympathetic whites and **free blacks** (see p. 23), where escaped slaves could be hidden. "Conductors," as these sympathizers were called, helped run-aways travel from one station to another. The fugitives settled in the U.S. North or continued on to Canada. Some went to Mexico or the Caribbean, where slavery had been abolished. It is estimated that thousands of African Americans left the South via the Underground Railroad.

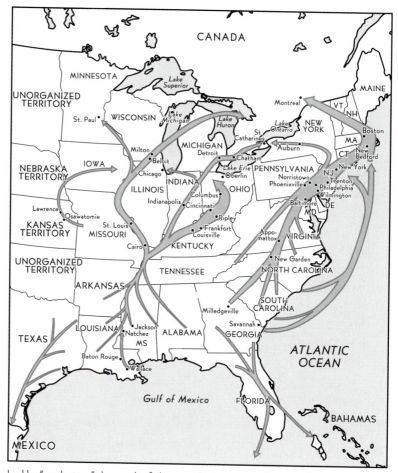

Led by "conductors," thousands of slaves made their way to freedom along the routes of the Underground Railroad.

Vesey Conspiracy

Denmark Vesey (ca. 1767–1822) was an enslaved person in South Carolina. In 1800, he won $1,500 in a lottery and bought his freedom. With the rest of the winnings he opened a carpentry shop in Charleston, South Carolina.

Even as a free black, Vesey was treated poorly. Vesey wanted to fight back and free enslaved African Americans. In 1822, he began to make plans for an attack on the city of Charleston. Some historians believe that as many as 9,000 blacks were involved in Vesey's plot.

Vesey's plan might have worked, but an enslaved person betrayed him. Vesey and 130 other African Americans were arrested. The court sentenced 35 African Americans, including Vesey, to death by hanging. Thirty-two were exiled to the

Great Escapes: Tales of the Underground Railroad

The Underground Railroad rescued thousands of slaves and helped them to freedom. Here are three of their stories.

Henry "Box" Brown, a slave in Virginia, is known for the most unusual method of escaping: he mailed himself north to freedom. He began his journey by stepping into a large box and having a friend nail it shut. All he took with him was a few biscuits and a little water. Air holes in the box allowed him to breath. Brown's friend addressed the box to another friend in Philadelphia and wrote on the box "This Side Up With Care." Twenty-six hours later, the box arrived in Philadelphia and Henry rose up in his box, reached out his hand, and said, "How do you do, gentlemen?"

Harriet Tubman helped so many African Americans escape slavery that she was known as "Moses," the deliverer of her people. She told an interviewer that there were rules that governed escapes. One rule was that if anyone gave up and threatened to go back, they were to be shot so as not to endanger the rest of the group. On one journey a man's sore and swollen feet hurt him so that he told Tubman that he would rather go back and die than go another step. The group tried to nurse his feet and get him moving, but he refused. Then Tubman gave the orders to have him shot: "I told the boys to get their guns ready, and shoot him. They'd have done it in a minute; but when he heard that, he jumped right up and went on as well as any body...."

Margaret Ward escaped from slavery with her infant son. Her owner sold Ward to a tobacco plantation owner in Louisiana while she was pregnant. Ward worked until the day her son was born. After giving birth, she returned to fields immediately. Ward was forced to leave her son under a bush and could visit him only twice a day. At the end of the day, Ward was horrified to see her baby was half-dead. After she revived him, she ran away. Ward made it to freedom. Her son, Samuel Ringgold Ward, became a speaker for the abolitionist movement.

Caribbean. Slave laws in South Carolina were strengthened in the years after the revolt.

Walker, David

David Walker was the son of an enslaved father and free African American mother. According to the law, because David Walker's mother was free, he was free. Walker witnessed so many enslaved Africans humiliated and abused that he left the South. He settled in Boston, but found that even in the North, African Americans were treated with prejudice. By 1828, Walker was a leading force in the fight to end slavery.

In 1829, Walker wrote the "Appeal to the Coloured Citizens of the World." In it Walker told enslaved people to take responsibility for their freedom and to revolt against their masters. Walker was one of the first to support revolts as a way of gaining freedom. Many were shocked. Georgian planters put a price of $3,000 for Walker dead and $10,000 if he could be brought in alive. Friends feared for his life and begged him to move to Canada. Walker refused. In June 1830, Walker was found dead in his home. Many were certain that he had been poisoned, but

Appeal to the Coloured Citizens of the World (1829)

David Walker, an African American abolitionist, published his Appeal in an effort to inspire enslaved African Americans to rise up and end slavery.

Having travelled over a considerable portion of these United States, and having, in the course of my travels, taken the most accurate observations of things as they exist—the result of my observations has warranted the full and unshaken conviction, that we, (coloured people of these United States,) are the most degraded, wretched, and abject set of beings that ever lived since the world began; and I pray God that none like us ever may live again until time shall be no more.

...I must observe to my brethren that at the close of the first Revolution in this country, with Great Britain, there were but thirteen States in the Union, now there are twenty-four, most of which are slaveholding States, and the whites are dragging us around in chains and in handcuffs, to their new States and Territories to work their mines and farms, to enrich them and their children—and millions of them believing firmly that we being a little darker than they, were made by our Creator to be an inheritance to them and their children for ever—the same as a parcel of brutes [animals].

Source: "David Walker's Appeal," in *Four Articles...,* rev. ed.

African Americans in the West

African Americans participated in the California gold rush, but few made their fortune in the mines. Most grew wealthy by providing services and goods that the miners needed.

Author	Narrative
Alvin Coffey	Alvin Coffey purchased his family's freedom and then moved west to California during the gold rush. Eventually, the Coffeys became wealthy owners of a northern California laundry business.
William Alexander Leidesdorff	A free African American, Leidesdorff became a successful merchant in San Francisco. He opened the first hotel in the growing city. In time he owned a 35,000-acre ranch and became a leader of the city. He died of fever in 1848.
Clara Brown	Virginia slave Clara Brown purchased her freedom and traveled to Colorado when gold was discovered there. She cooked and washed for the miners, making enough money to bring many of her relatives to Colorado after the Civil War. Brown invested in mines and soon became one of the wealthiest people in Colorado.
Mifflin Gibbs	Gibbs, a free African American, traveled to California during the gold rush. He opened a clothing store and founded a newspaper. Gibbs left California in 1858 and studied at Oberlin College. He later became a lawyer and a judge in Arkansas.

could not find evidence of the crime. Some historians believe that Walker may have died of tuberculosis, a disease that had killed his daughter.

Western Expansion

During the first half of the 19th century, the United States gained vast amounts of new territory in the West. After the Louisiana Purchase in 1803, fur trappers became some of the first explorers to travel the West. One of the first was an African American named **James Beckwourth** (see p. 76). After the U.S.-Mexican War (1846–1848), the United States gained new territories. Americans moved west to look for new opportunities. African Americans were among those who wanted to build a new life in the West.

In 1849, tens of thousands of people rushed to California when gold was discovered. During the California gold rush about

2,000 **free blacks** (see p. 23) came looking for fortune. A gold rush in Colorado drew African Americans as well.

A number of enslaved Africans came west with their masters. All hoped for economic and social freedom. California passed laws that limited African American freedom. African Americans could not testify in court and could not vote. African Americans fought against these laws and during the **Civil War** (see p. 108) they were repealed.

CHAPTER FOUR

Free at Last

The Civil War and Reconstruction, 1861–1876

"Let the black man get upon his person the brass letters 'U.S.,' let him get an eagle on his buttons and a musket on his shoulder and there is no power on earth which can deny that he has earned the right to citizenship in the United States."

—Frederick Douglass

Throughout the 1850s, tensions between the North and the South rose. One of the main conflicts was over the issue of slavery. In 1861, the southern states seceded, or broke away, from the Union to form the **Confederate States of America** (see p. 110). A civil war tore the United States apart from 1861 until 1865. President **Abraham Lincoln** (see pp. 85, 119) said that the **Civil War** (see p. 108) was fought to keep the nation united, not to end slavery. The South said it fought to protect states' rights to govern themselves. African Americans thought of the conflict as a "freedom war." The simple truth is that without slavery, there would have been no war. And without that war, there would have been no end to slavery (see **emancipation**, p. 113).

AFRICAN AMERICANS IN THE CIVIL WAR

Throughout the Civil War, the future of African Americans was uncertain. They had nothing to say about the war. Those African Americans who lived in the North were kept out of government. Most of the African Americans in the South were still enslaved. Yet once war broke out, African Americans were eager to take part. Thousands fled behind Union lines. Unfortunately, the Union was not ready to accept them. For the war's first year,

African Americans worked as Union mule drivers, cooks, attendants, and waiters. They were not permitted to be soldiers. It would not be until later in the war that African Americans were allowed to fight.

In the South, runaway enslaved people led Union soldiers to hidden supplies of food and cotton. Some African American women worked as Union

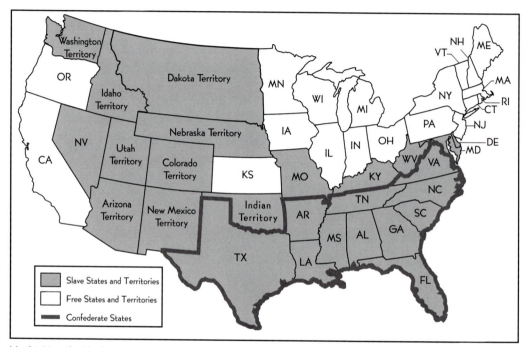

Until 1861, the North and South preserved a delicate balance between free and slave states.

Timeline

1861–1865

The **Civil War** is fought between the North and the 11 southern states, over the issue of slavery. The southern states form the **Confederate States of America**.

1861

The First **Confiscation Act** prohibits the return of slaves who escape to Union lines. Because slave owners considered enslaved Africans to be property, Congress decided that confiscating, or taking away, that "property" was legal in war.

spies. **Abolitionists** (see pp. 45, 73) like **Harriet Tubman** (see p. 89) used their **Underground Railroad** (see p. 91) connections to spy and help Union troops. Tubman later recruited former slaves as soldiers for the Union Army.

A GRADUAL EMANCIPATION

The first free black troops joined the army in 1862. This was after Congress banned slavery in Washington, D.C., and the territories. Lincoln resisted pressure to free all slaves. He was afraid the slaveholding states of Missouri, Kentucky, Delaware, and Maryland would leave the Union and join the rebels.

Finally on January 1, 1863, Lincoln's **Emancipation Proclamation** (see p. 113) took effect. It freed enslaved Africans only in areas in rebellion. In May, the Louisiana Colored Volunteers took part in the battle of Port Hudson, Louisiana. In July black regiments from Massachusetts fought heroically at Fort Wagner, South Carolina. Eventually, African American troops made up nearly 10 percent of the Union Army.

African Americans played major roles in the Union Navy, too. By war's end, one in four Union sailors was African American. Eight African Americans won the navy's medal of honor and 15 won the army's.

UNREST, NORTH AND SOUTH

In the North, many whites did not like fighting for African American freedom. Struggling to find work, they were afraid freed slaves would compete

1861	1862	1863	1863
Charlotte Forten travels to the islands off of South Carolina after the Union Army captures the islands early in the war. Once there, she helps found the Penn School, and other schools for newly freed African Americans.	Congress passes the **Morrill Land Grant Act**, which gives money to all loyal Union states to build public colleges on federal land. After the act is extended to the southern states in 1890, all-black schools such as Tuskegee Institute open.	**Abraham Lincoln** issues the Emancipation Proclamation, freeing slaves in Confederate-held territory and authorizing the use of African Americans in the Union Army. Thousands of African Americans enroll in the army.	The Conscription Act, allowing for the first draft of soldiers in U.S. history, sparks **race riots** in several large cities. The worst riot occurs in New York City in July.

for jobs. Poor whites were also angry that rich whites could buy their way out of military service. In July 1863, there were riots in New York City to protest the draft (see **race riots**, p 122). Other riots followed in Boston, Albany, Chicago, Cleveland, and Detroit.

On southern plantations, owners tried to keep emancipation secret. The rebels said if they captured any African American soldiers, they would be enslaved and their white officers executed. Still, thousands of African Americans enlisted in the Union Army.

WAR'S END BRINGS NEW WOES

The year 1865 brought both great joy and great pain. On April 4, Lincoln visited the captured Confederate capital of Richmond, Virginia. Joyfully weeping African Americans lined the streets to express their thanks. A week later, the president was shot by John Wilkes Booth, an unhappy southerner, and died on April 15. Now the crowds wept in mourning. Also in 1865, the 13th Amendment to the Constitution ended slavery everywhere. For the next dozen years, the nation struggled with two huge problems. One was how to feed, clothe, and educate 4 million newly freed African Americans and find a new place in society for them. The second was what punishment, if any, would be given to former Confederates.

If ever the nation needed Lincoln's wisdom, it was now. However, Lincoln's successor, President Andrew Johnson, was a stubborn man without

1863	1864	1865	1865
Fanny Kemble's diary, *Journal of a Residence on a Georgia Plantation*, is published. The diary, written by the wife of a plantation owner, describes the conditions of slave life in the South.	In the **Fort Pillow Massacre** hundreds of African American and white Union soldiers are slaughtered by Confederate troops. African American women and children are also killed.	After winning a second term and ending the Civil War, President **Abraham Lincoln** is assassinated.	Southern states begin passing **Black Codes**, laws that discriminate against African Americans. The 13th Amendment prohibits slavery.

Lincoln's patience and political skills. He was from Tennessee, but Johnson had voted against his state joining the the Confederacy when the war broke out. Now he sympathized with defeated white southerners.

RECONSTRUCTION BEGINS

After the war southern legislatures nearly re-created slavery. The so-called **Black Codes** (see p. 105) bound former slaves to *apprenticeship* programs. Any rulebreaking was made a crime. Many members of Congress were outraged. A committee called the Joint Committee on Reconstruction was formed to investigate unfair treatment of newly freed African Americans. The period that followed became known as **Reconstruction** (see p. 123).

The goals of the Reconstruction period varied. President Johnson and some in Congress wanted to welcome the former Confederate states back into the Union without punishing them. Others wanted harsher measures taken against the former Confederacy. They also wanted to help newly freed African Americans. The most radical, led by Senator **Thaddeus Stevens** (see p. 125) of Pennsylvania, wanted to divide Confederate property among former enslaved Africans. The radicals agreed with the Union general William T. Sherman, who had said that every freedman should be awarded **"forty acres and a mule"** (see p. 116).

Republicans wasted no time in passing legislation. The 14th Amendment to the Constitution (see **amendments to the U.S. Constitution**,

1866	**1866**	**1868**	**1868**
The **Freedmen's Bureau** is opened.	**Ku Klux Klan**, a violent racist organization, is founded.	The First **Reconstruction Act** is passed, dividing the South into military districts and making readmission into the Union more difficult.	The 14th Amendment grants citizenship to anyone born in the United States. **Race riots** break out in several cities in Louisiana.

p. 105) said that the Constitution applied to everyone, regardless of race, and that states could not limit those rights. The 15th Amendment said that race would not be a consideration for voting. A series of **civil rights acts** (see p. 107) provided other protections. Other acts put the South under military rule. The **Freedmen's Bureau** (see p. 117) was set up to help freed slaves build new lives. Hundreds of Freedmen's schools were built to educate former slaves (also see **education**, p. 111). After the Union captured the estate of Confederate General Robert E. Lee, **Freedmen's Village** (see p. 117), including a school, homes, a church, a hospital, and shops, was built on the property.

President Johnson vetoed laws whenever he could, but Congress overrode his vetoes. When his secretary of war sided with the Republicans, Johnson fired him. Because there was a new law forbidding firing a *cabinet member* without the approval of Congress, Johnson was impeached. When the impeachment reached the Senate, the president was acquitted by one vote, but after his trial he had little power.

A BRIEF EMPOWERMENT

Beginning in 1867, African American men truly shared in the political process. Some 700,000 registered to vote. In Washington, D.C., Missouri, and in every state of the old Confederacy, blacks held office. More than 1,500 were elected or appointed to state and local offices. Free-born Hiram Revels

1868	1870	1870	1871
Union Army commander General Ulysses S. Grant is elected president with help from African American voters.	Senator Hiram R. Revels of Mississippi and Representative Joseph H. Rainey of South Carolina become the first African American members of Congress.	The 15th Amendment makes it illegal to deny anyone the vote based on race, color, or past servitude.	The **Fisk Jubilee Singers**, a singing group founded to raise money for Fisk University, begins a nationwide tour. Their popularity helps spread spiritual music throughout the United States.

and formerly enslaved Blanche K. Bruce were elected to the U.S. Senate. Fourteen other African Americans served in the House of Representatives.

Although white opponents portrayed **African American politicians** (see p. 122) as uneducated and easily fooled, most were not. Many had been born free or gained freedom before the war. In South Carolina, Louisiana and Virginia, they often came from wealthy, educated families. Others were skilled laborers such as carpenters or *blacksmiths*, whose work had often taken them into the larger society. Still others were teachers, journalists, or ministers.

Still, many whites would not accept the idea that former slaves should have political and property rights. Many whites had owned no slaves, but now they felt threatened by freed blacks. Sometimes wealthy planters joined poor and working-class whites to keep blacks in place.

Some groups from all classes took the law into their own hands. They threatened and sometimes killed African Americans and the whites who sided with them. The **Ku Klux Klan** (see p. 118) became the most famous of these groups. Its riders wore white sheets and hoods to hide their identity. But often it was known who they were. Their goal was to threaten blacks and their white supporters, and defeat black officeholders and the northerners who had come to rebuild the South.

Former Union General Ulysses S. Grant followed Johnson as president. He supported laws to fight the Ku Klux Klan. He sent federal troops into South Carolina and ordered arrests of people who had been terrorizing

1871	**1872**	**1874**	**1874**
The **Ku Klux Klan** Act allows federal troops to arrest members of the Klan.	President Grant wins re-election, defeating newspaper editor and former abolitionist **Horace Greeley**.	The Freedmen's Bureau is closed. P. B. S. Pinchback becomes the first African American governor in Louisiana.	Blanche K. Bruce is elected to the U.S. Senate and becomes the first African American to complete a six-year term in the Senate.

blacks. Radical Republicans had one last victory in the Civil Rights Act of 1875. It integrated hotels, theaters, and restaurants in the South. The law was poorly enforced, and in 1883, the Supreme Court ruled it unconstitutional. Sadly, it would take about 80 years to restore those rights.

President Grant's two terms were marked by scandal after scandal. Although personally honest, he could not stop the corruption that existed in the nation. The election of 1876, between Democrat Samuel Tilden and Republican Rutherford B. Hayes, gave Tilden the popular vote. But 20 electoral votes were in doubt. When a special election commission gave the votes and the presidency to Hayes, the South threatened to leave the Union again.

To satisfy white southern Democrats, Hayes made a deal. He agreed to withdraw federal troops from the South and build up its industry. This marked the end of Reconstruction. The federal government would no longer ensure that African Americans would be treated justly. Many would flee to the West, but most African Americans chose to stay. They continued to farm, working for white landowners as **sharecroppers** (see p. 124). Sharecropping was not an easy life, but it was an improvement over slavery.

1875   1876   1877

The **Civil Rights Act** of 1875 prohibits discrimination in public places. It was struck down as unconstitutional in 1883.

In *United States v. Cruikshank*, the Supreme Court decides that the states decide which of their citizens may vote and under which conditions. The decision undercuts voting rights for African Americans.

The disputed presidential election of Rutherford B. Hayes and Samuel Tilden ends **Reconstruction** when Hayes is made president.

A-Z of Key People, Events, and Terms

amendments to the U.S. Constitution

The years after the Civil War were known as the **Reconstruction** (see p. 123) period. During this time, several amendments were added to the U.S. Constitution. These amendments guaranteed certain rights to Americans of all races and colors. The 13th Amendment was passed in 1865. It banned slavery in the United States. The 14th Amendment was passed in 1868. It gave citizenship to all persons born in the United States, including African Americans. Passed in 1870, the 15th Amendment forbade states to deny any male citizen the right to vote based on "race, color or previous condition of servitude."

American Missionary Association (AMA)

The American Missionary Association was founded in 1846. It opened schools and churches in the South during the **Civil War** (see p. 108) and **Reconstruction** (see p. 123) eras. Mary S. Peake founded one of these schools in Hampton, Virginia. This was the first black public school in the South. This school was later called Hampton Institute. Later the AMA opened schools in North Carolina and other southern states.

After the war, the AMA continued to open schools to educate freed Africans. By 1868, more than 500 AMA teachers and *missionaries* were working throughout the South. White AMA teachers did not respect African American culture. In fact, some teachers held racist views. Still, the AMA accomplished a great deal. It established a number of colleges and universities for African Americans. These included Fisk University, Berea College, Atlanta University, Talladega College, Hampton Institute, and LeMoyne Institute. (Also see **education**, p. 111, and **Fisk Jubilee Singers**, p. 115.)

Black Codes

After the **Civil War** (see p. 108), southern states passed laws called "Black Codes." These laws greatly limited the freedom of

Constitutional Amendments Passed during Reconstruction

During the Reconstruction era (1865–1876), three key amendments to the U.S. Constitution were passed. These amendments gave all Americans rights of citizenship, regardless of race or color. African American men were given the right to vote. However, women, black and white, would not gain this right until 1920.

13th Amendment (Passed by Congress January 31, 1865. Ratified by States December 6, 1865.)

• Forbids slavery and involuntary servitude (labor).

• Allows prisoners to be made to work.

South's Reaction: Mississippi did not officially ratify this amendment until 1995.

14th Amendment (Passed by Congress June 13, 1866. Ratified by States July 9, 1868.)

• Guarantees citizenship to all those born or naturalized in the United States. In the past, African Americans—enslaved or free—had been denied citizenship.

• States that all citizens are protected by U.S. laws and are entitled to due process of law.

• Provides that state representation in Congress is based on the number of people in the state. This replaced the three-fifths clause (see **U.S. Constitution**, p. 62).

• Penalizes those states that do not allow all qualified male citizens to vote by reducing the number of the state's representatives in Congress.

• Prohibits people who had been federal or state officials before the Civil War and who had joined the Confederacy from serving as government officials. In 1872, Congress reversed this rule.

• Prohibits payment to former slave owners for the loss of their slaves.

South's Reaction: At first, most southern states refused to ratify this amendment. They ratified it only when the Radical Republicans in Congress made readmission dependent on ratification of this amendment. After passage of the amendment, segregated facilities for blacks and whites began appearing in the South.

15th Amendment (Passed by Congress February 26, 1869. Ratified by States on February 2, 1870.)

• Gives all male citizens the right to vote.

South's Reaction: A variety of regulations arose in the South to prevent African Americans from voting.

African Americans. Political and economic power was kept in the hands of whites. Each state passed its own set of laws, but all Black Codes intended to take away African Americans' civil rights and to control their lives.

Mississippi and South Carolina passed the first Black Codes in late 1865. Other southern states soon followed. The laws of each state contained many of the same principles: African Americans could rent land only in rural areas. All African Americans were required to sign annual contracts for employment each January. If they quit before they completed a year's work, they lost any wages they had earned. They could also be arrested. African Americans could be whipped, fined, or made to perform forced labor if they did not have a job. African Americans were not allowed to "insult" whites. They had to have a license to preach. Some codes did not permit black women to be homemakers. They had to work in the fields. In reaction, Congress passed the **civil rights acts** (see below) of 1866 over President Andrew Johnson's *veto*.

civil rights acts

Congress passed a number of civil rights acts during the **Reconstruction** (see p. 123) era. The Civil Rights Act of 1866 guaranteed citizenship and equal legal rights to African Americans. President Andrew Johnson used his *veto* to try to stop the bill, but Congress overrode him. African Americans were given the right to make contracts, testify in court, and hold property. The act supported the 14th Amendment to the Constitution (See **amendments to the U.S. Constitution**, p. 105.)

The Civil Rights Act of 1875 made discrimination illegal in public places. It gave African Americans the right to sue and receive damages from anyone who broke the law. A number of lawsuits were filed. In the end, the Supreme Court had to decide if the law was constitutional.

In 1883, the Supreme Court ruled the civil rights acts to be unconstitutional. The Court decided that Congress could not regulate the social customs of a state. Congress had no power over individual citizens who discriminated against each other. The Court's ruling meant that the 14th Amendment applied to acts of the state governments, not to individuals or to corporations.

Civil War

The Civil War was America's bloodiest war. The northern states, called the Union, fought against the southern states that had left the Union. The southern states had established the **Confederate States of America** (see p. 110). This was also called the Confederacy. Tensions had been building between the North and South years before war broke out. The main issues were slavery and political power. As the United States spread westward, the South wanted slavery to move west also. The North was against this. **Abraham Lincoln** (see p. 119) was elected president in 1860. He tried to convince the South that he did not plan to end slavery where it already existed. Lincoln wanted to keep slavery from spreading west. However, the southern states still believed that Lincoln would end slavery. In response, between 1860 and 1861, eleven southern states left the Union.

The first shots of the Civil War were fired at Fort Sumter, South Carolina, on April 12, 1861. This caused many men to join either the Union or Confederate army. African Americans tried to volunteer to serve as soldiers in the Union Army. They were turned down. At that time black volunteers could serve only as camp attendants, waiters, and cooks.

One of the first African American regiments in the Union Army was the 1st South Carolina Volunteers. General David Hunter formed them in May 1862. The 54th Massachusetts Regiment was also made up of free African Americans. Robert Gould Shaw commanded the *regiment*. He was a white abolitionist. In July 1863, the 54th saw combat at Fort Wagner, South Carolina. The 54th held the fort for nearly an hour before the Confederates pushed them out. The fighting was fierce. The regiment lost about half its men, including Colonel Shaw, but it won the admiration of the Union Army.

During the war, enslaved African Americans fled to the Union side. A total of about half a million ended up in Union camps. At least 200,000 served as cooks, carpenters, laborers, and nurses. The Union called escaped slaves "contraband." This meant property that was confiscated or seized from the enemy. This classified them as property instead of human beings. The Union refused to return enslaved Africans to their former owners. Congress passed

The all-African American troops of the 54th Massachusetts Regiment stormed the Confederate forces at Fort Wagner in 1863. Although the Confederates won the battle, the bravery of the black Union soldiers convinced many whites that African Americans were worthy of fighting for the Union. (Library of Congress)

Confiscation (*con-fis-CA-shun*) **Acts** (see p. 110) that freed any runaway enslaved person working for the Union Army.

The Confederate Army also used African American labor. Enslaved African Americans were forced to work on the railroad, in weapons factories, on farms, and other jobs. As the war went on, more enslaved people crossed Union lines and gained freedom.

By the middle of 1862, the Union Army had lost many battles. The government decided to allow African Americans to enlist as soldiers. More than 175,000 African Americans joined the Union Army and 29,000 joined the Union Navy. Many African Americans served the Union as spies. They could slip into Confederate territory pretending to be enslaved. About 10 percent of the Union Army was made up of African Americans. African Americans were only about one percent of the North's total population.

This did not mean African American soldiers were treated as equals. They were kept in segregated camps, given the worst jobs, and paid less than white soldiers. Still, African American soldiers won the respect of their white commanders and fellow soldiers. They were brave under fire and helped the North win victory.

Confederate States of America

On February 4, 1861, delegates from southern states that had left the Union met. They formed a nation they called the Confederate States of America. This included the states of South Carolina, Mississippi, Florida, Alabama, Georgia, Louisiana, Texas, Virginia, Arkansas, North Carolina, and Tennessee. The capital of the Confederacy was in Richmond, Virginia. **Jefferson Davis** (see p. 111) was the president of the Confederacy and Alexander Stephens its vice president. In March 1861, Stephens summed up the ideals of the Confederacy when he said, "Our new government is founded upon the great truth that the Negro is not equal to the white man; that slavery-subordination [inferiority] to the superior race is his natural and normal condition."

Confiscation Acts

The Confiscation Acts of 1861 and 1862 were laws passed by Congress during the **Civil War** (see p. 108). The First Confiscation Act allowed Union troops to take any property that was used to help the Confederacy rebel. It also forbade the return of runaway slaves. It made the United States responsible for the care of runaways.

The Second Confiscation Act freed all enslaved Africans who fought for the North. It also allowed the Union Army to give arms to African American soldiers.

Coppin, Fanny Jackson

Fanny Jackson Coppin (1837–1913) was born into slavery in Washington, D.C. When she was a young girl, her aunt bought her freedom. She moved to Rhode Island, where she worked as a servant. Coppin learned to read and write. She later went to Oberlin College in Ohio. In 1865, she received a bachelor's degree. This was rare for a woman—especially an African American woman. She was hired by the Institute for Colored Youth in Philadelphia. She later became its principal. She worked at the Institute for 37 years, teaching some of the future leaders of the African American community.

Coppin began a teacher-training program at the school. There was also an industrial department to train African Americans in the trades. The Institute was renamed Cheyney

University in 1902, when it was moved to Cheyney, Pennsylvania. It still exists today, and many consider it the first African American college.

Davis, Jefferson

Jefferson Davis (1808–1889) was president of the **Confederate States of America** (see p. 110) from 1861 to 1865. Davis supported states' rights and expansion of slavery into western territories. After the war, Davis was convicted of *treason* and was imprisoned in Fort Monroe, Virginia. He was released in May 1867.

education

During the **Civil War** (see p. 108) and **Reconstruction** (see p. 123), schools were opened throughout the South. Public elementary schools as well as schools of higher education were founded. Free African Americans taught newly freed people. Mary S. Peake, a free black woman working with the **American Missionary Association** (see p. 105), opened the first African

An African American Teacher's Opinion

During and after the Civil War, more than 9,000 teachers—both white and black—taught newly freed African Americans in the South. Here is how one African American teacher described the meaning of education to former slaves.

There is one woman who supports three children and keeps them at school; she says, "I don't care how hard I has to work, if I can only sen[d] Sallie and the boys to school looking respectable." Many of the girls have but one decent dress; it gets washed and ironed on Saturday, and then is worn until the next Saturday, provided they do not tear it or fall in the mud; when such an accident happens there is an absent mark on the register. ... One may go into their cabins on cold, windy days, and see daylight between the roof; but a word of complaint is rarely heard. They are anxious to have the children "get on" in their books, and do not seem to feel impatient if they lack comforts themselves. A pile of books is seen in almost every cabin, though there be no furniture except a poor bed, a table and two or three broken chairs.

Source: *Black Saga: The African American Experience.*

Freedmen's schools offered education to African American children as well as adults.
(Library of Congress)

American public school in 1861. This was in Hampton, Virginia. After the war, the school became Hampton Institute. This was one of the first African American colleges.

Some newly freed people began schools in South Carolina and Virginia during the war. Susie King Taylor was a runaway slave from South Carolina. She taught African American soldiers. Her husband was a soldier in an all-black regiment.

In the North, African Americans who attended school usually went to segregated schools. These served only African Americans. One example of a segregated school was the Institute for Colored Youth in Philadephia, which would be led after the war by **Fanny Jackson Coppin** (see p. 110). Not all northern schools were segregated, however. In 1855, the Boston public schools served both blacks and whites. These were the first integrated schools.

After the Civil War, the **Freedmen's Bureau** (see p. 117) established thousands of schools in the South for both children and adults. By the 1870s, about 25 percent of school-age former slaves were attending public schools. However, when **Reconstruction** (see p. 123) ended, white southerners tried to stop efforts to educate African Americans.

emancipation

Emancipation is the freeing of enslaved African Americans. During the **Civil War** (see p. 108), many argued over emancipation. Black and white abolitionists supported immediate emancipation of all enslaved African Americans. Those who did not support emancipation included slaveholders in the border states. These were states that were part of the Union, but were located along the Confederate border. Many white laborers did not want to see enslaved African Americans set free because they were afraid that free blacks would compete with whites for jobs.

To maintain support for the war, **Abraham Lincoln** (see pp. 85, 119) had to balance the desires of all these groups. From the war's start, Lincoln said that his main goal was to bring the southern states back into the Union. Several of Lincoln's generals tried to free enslaved African Americans in the parts of the South they controlled. General John C. Frémont issued a proclamation in 1861 freeing Missouri slaves. President Lincoln rejected Frémont's proclamation and removed him from his command. General David Hunter tried to free slaves in Confederate-held areas in South Carolina, Georgia, and Florida in 1863. Lincoln also rejected Hunter's proclamation. Finally, in 1862, Lincoln issued the **Emancipation Proclamation** (see below).

Juneteenth

Juneteenth celebrates the reading of the Emancipation Proclamation in Galveston, Texas. Some southern slaveholders would not tell their enslaved peoples they were free. As Union troops advanced, news of the Emancipation Proclamation spread. In Galveston, enslaved people did not get the news until June 1865. African Americans in the Galveston area celebrated "Juneteenth" as a holiday of freedom. On January 1, 1980, Texas made Juneteenth an official state holiday. Today, Juneteenth is also celebrated in other parts of the country. It is a celebration of freedom from slavery and respect for all cultures.

Emancipation Proclamation

President **Abraham Lincoln** (see pp. 85, 119) issued the Emancipation Proclamation on January 1, 1863. This document freed enslaved African Americans who were in states or regions that were fighting against the Union.

Several events led to Lincoln's decision. In April 1862, Lincoln signed a bill that freed all enslaved African Americans in

Emancipation Proclamation (1863)

On January 1, 1863, President Abraham Lincoln issued the Emancipation Proclamation. It freed enslaved African Americans who were in places still held by the Confederate Army on that date. It did not free slaves who lived in border states loyal to the Union or in areas in the South held by the Union Army. Still, it was recognized as a document of freedom. Below is an excerpt from the Emancipation Proclamation.

That on the 1st day of January, A.D. 1863, all persons held as slaves within any State or designated part of a State the people whereof shall then be in rebellion against the United States shall be then, thenceforward, and forever free; and the executive government of the United States, including the military and naval authority thereof, will recognize and maintain the freedom of such persons and will do no act or acts to repress such persons, or any of them, in any efforts they may make for their actual freedom. ...

And I hereby enjoin upon the people so declared to be free to abstain from all violence, unless in necessary self-defense; and I recommend to them that, in all case when allowed, they labor faithfully for reasonable wages.

And I further declare and make known that such persons of suitable condition will be received into the armed service of the United States to garrison forts, positions, stations, and other places, and to man vessels of all sorts in said service.

Source: National Archives.

Washington, D.C. Part of the bill set aside funds to pay passage for African Americans who wished to go to Haiti. Lincoln supported colonization because he did not believe that African Americans and whites could live together. In June 1862 Lincoln freed slaves in all the territories west of the Mississippi. Soon after, a law freed those who escaped from Confederate slaveholders.

In 1862 the Union won a victory at Antietam, Maryland. After this, Lincoln issued the Emancipation Proclamation. The Proclamation did not free all enslaved peoples. It freed only those in areas that were still fighting against the United States. Historians point out that since the Confederacy was not under Lincoln's control, he really freed no one. Yet, free and enslaved African Americans celebrated when the Emancipation

Proclamation was issued. They understood that it was a step toward true freedom.

Fisk Jubilee Singers

The Fisk Jubilee Singers sang *spirituals* and religious songs to raise money for Fisk University. The university was founded in 1867 in Nashville, Tennessee. Its mission was to educate newly freed enslaved blacks. In the early 1870s the school was in financial trouble. The school's administrators thought a series of concerts would raise the money needed to maintain the school.

The Fisk Jubilee Singers began in 1871 with a tour of the United States. Their popularity helped spread spiritual music throughout the United States and Europe. The Jubilee Singers toured Great Britain and other European countries from 1873 to 1878. They were successful in raising money for a number of buildings. These are still a large part of Fisk University.

Forten, Charlotte

Charlotte Forten (1837–1914) was the granddaughter of **James Forten** (see p. 56). She attended integrated schools in Massachusetts. She became the first African American women to teach white students in Massachusetts. When the **Civil War** (see p. 108) broke out, Charlotte Forten went to the Sea Islands off South Carolina's coast. There she set up schools to teach former slaves. She enrolled thousands of children in school and began to teach adults to read. She stayed on the islands until 1864. After the war, she worked as a clerk for the U.S. Treasury, and later married.

Fort Pillow Massacre

Fort Pillow was located on the Mississippi River about 40 miles north of Memphis, Tennessee. The Union Army had captured the fort from the Confederates. Major Lionel F. Booth commanded the fort for the Union. Two hundred and ninety-five white Tennessee troops and 262 African American troops defended it.

On April 12, 1864, a Confederate force led by Nathan Bedford Forrest (see **Ku Klux Klan**, p. 118) captured the fort.

The Fort Pillow Massacre: Survivors Speak (1864)

General Forrest, who later became a founder of the Ku Klux Klan, denied that a massacre took place. However, a congressional investigation indicated otherwise. In the first excerpt, an African American survivor of the battle reports what he saw. The second excerpt contains part of Lieutenant Mack J. Leaming's report to Congress.

Most all the men that were killed on our side were killed after the fight was over. They called them out and shot them down. Then they put some in the houses and shut them up, and then burned the houses.

The bravery of our troops in the defense of Fort Pillow, I think, cannot be questioned. Many of the men, and particularly the colored soldiers, had never before been under fire; yet every man did his duty with a courage and determined resolution, seldom if ever surpassed in similar engagements. Had Forrest not violated the rules of civilized warfare in taking advantage of the flag of truce in the manner I have mentioned in another part of this report, I am confident we could have held the fort against all his assaults during the day, when, if we had been properly supported during the night by the major-general commanding at Memphis, a glorious victory to the Union cause would have been the result of the next day's operations.

Source: Library of Congress.

Forrest's troops took few prisoners. Upon entering the fort they killed 90 percent of the African Americans, including women and children. About 80 percent of white Union soldiers were also killed.

"forty acres and a mule"

Union General William T. Sherman first used the slogan "forty acres and a mule." In 1865, Sherman recommended that all former African American slaves receive forty acres of land and a mule from the government. According to Sherman's plan, the land would come from plantations of defeated white slaveowners. He wanted to divide the Sea Islands and a small section of land that stretched along the southern coast from Charleston, South Carolina. Sadly, most African Americans did not get any land.

Freedmen's Bureau

The U.S. Congress established the Freedmen's Bureau in March 1865. It was responsible for protecting the rights of 4 million freed slaves, restoring civil law as the war ended, and feeding and clothing freed enslaved people. It also provided services to white war refugees. The Bureau established schools, hospitals, and churches. It rented out plantation lands to African Americans. It also created and enforced sharecropping contracts between black workers and white planters. By war's end the bureau had settled some 10,000 black and white families on plantation lands that had been taken over.

Northerners and Southerners opposed the Freedmen's Bureau. Northerners felt that once enslaved African Americans were freed, they didn't need help from the government. Southerners did not want Northerners to aid their former slaves.

The Freedmen's Bureau provided African Americans with legal support **education** (see p. 111). The Freedmen's Bureau operated over 2,000 schools.

Freedmen's Village

This village was founded in the summer of 1863 on Confederate General Robert E. Lee's estate. The North took this property after the war. The community offered escaped slaves shelter and the chance to build a better life. The villagers built homes, a church, a hospital, a school, and businesses. They farmed the land, and by the end of 1863 had earned profits of $60,000. Freedmen's Village existed until 1900, when the U.S. government forced it to close.

Greeley, Horace

Horace Greeley (1811-1872) was a well-known journalist and abolitionist. In 1841, he founded the *New York Tribune*. He was editor of this newspaper for more than 30 years.

Greeley was against slavery, alcohol, gambling, and *capital punishment*. Greeley was a strong supporter of the Free Soil Party and helped form the **Republican Party** (see p. 87) in 1856. He supported **Abraham Lincoln**'s (see pp. 85, 119) campaign for the presidency. He wanted Lincoln to completely abolish slavery.

After the **Civil War** (see p. 108), Greeley joined the Radical Republicans and helped form a new party. This was the Liberal

Republican Party. In 1872, Greeley ran for president against Ulysses S. Grant. Greeley lost the election, but won 40 percent of the popular vote. A few weeks after the election, Greeley died.

Kemble, Frances Anne (Fanny)

Fanny Kemble was born in London, England, in 1809. She was an actress, a writer, and a musician. She met Pierce Butler in 1832 when she was working in the theater in America. The Butler family were among the biggest slave owners in the United States. Butler and Kemble fell in love and married in 1834. Despite Butler's attempts to persuade her of the benefits of slavery, Kemble remained an abolitionist.

Kemble finally visited one of her husband's plantations and was horrified at the conditions. Her record of her visit is one of the few firsthand accounts of plantation life from an abolitionist's point of view. She did not publish her journal until 1863. *Journal of a Residence on a Georgian Plantation* was published in Britain to convince the nation to support the North in the **Civil War** (see p. 108). It was published in the United States the same year.

The Ku Klux Klan: A History of Violence and Racism

Below are the recollections of a former slave about the activities of the Ku Klux Klan.

The government built schoolhouses, and the Ku Klux Klan went to work and burned 'em down.... The Ku Kluxes ... wore long sheets and covered the horses with sheets so you couldn't recognize 'em. Men you thought was your friends was Ku Kluxes, and you'd deal with them in stores in the daytime, and at night they'd come out to your house and kill you.

Source: Library of Congress.

Ku Klux Klan (KKK)

The Ku Klux Klan, a violent racist organization, was formed in 1866. Its goal was to establish white power throughout the South. Former Confederate general Nathan Bedford Forrest led the KKK. He was the same general who had led the **Fort Pillow Massacre** (see p. 115) in 1864. By 1877, the KKK had established groups in every southern state.

Most Klan members were poor southern whites. Planters, merchants, and Democratic Party officials were its leaders. The Klan became known for its violent acts against African Americans and their Republican supporters. The Klan especially targeted African

American **Civil War** (see p. 108) veterans, and politically active or economically successful blacks. Dressed in white hoods and body sheets, the Klan would attack mostly at night. They frightened, beat, and abused African Americans and their supporters. They burned homes, schools, and businesses. Once **Reconstruction** (see p. 123) ended, the Klan's activities increased.

Ku Klux Klan members. (Library of Congress)

To try to end the Klan's actions, Congress passed the Enforcement, or Ku Klux Klan, Acts in 1870 and 1871. These laws gave federal officials more control over voter registration and the election process. They put in place penalties for those who tried to take away voting rights. Under these laws, thousands of Klan members were charged with crimes. About 2,000 Klansmen were driven out of South Carolina. However, attempts to end the Klan's actions rarely worked. Most white southerners supported the Klan and refused to testify against its members in court. White juries would not convict those accused of violence against African Americans. Only about 600 Klansmen were convicted and sent to jail. Those convicted served only short jail terms.

The Klan may have killed as many as 10,000 southerners between the late 1860s and the end of Reconstruction. Although the Klan exists today, its power is much reduced. It faces more severe penalties for illegal racially motivated actions.

Lincoln, Abraham

Abraham Lincoln (1809–1865) was the 16th president of the United States. Lincoln was elected in 1860 and again in 1864. Lincoln led the nation during the **Civil War** (see p. 108). When the Confederacy left the Union, Lincoln saw the restoration of the Union as his main goal. Although pressured by white and black abolitionists, Lincoln did not free all enslaved blacks during the

Abraham Lincoln: Objectives of the Civil War

In a letter to Horace Greeley, dated August 22, 1862, Abraham Lincoln summed up his objectives in the war and his feelings about freeing the slaves.

If there be those who would not save the Union unless they could at the same time destroy slavery, I do not agree with them. My paramount object in this struggle is to save the Union, and is not either to save or destroy slavery. If I could save the Union without freeing any slave, I would do it; and if I could save it by freeing all the slaves, I would do it; and if I could do it by freeing some and leaving others alone, I would also do that.

Source: National Archives.

war. He believed that doing so would cause the North and South never to be able to come together peacefully.

In 1863, Lincoln issued the **Emancipation Proclamation** (see p. 113). Most freed Africans held Lincoln in high regard.

Lincoln's death filled African American communities with grief. One African American soldier recalled, "It was the gloomiest day I ever saw." Another wrote, "Ah! Never was a man so widely mourned before. The whole world bowed their heads in grief when Abraham Lincoln died." (See also **Abraham Lincoln**, pp. 85, 119.)

military, African Americans in

When the **Civil War** (see p. 108) broke out, African Americans were not allowed to join the Union Army. Leaders such as Frederick Douglass tried to convince the government to reverse the decision. When the U.S. government opened enlistment to blacks, Douglass encouraged African Americans to join. Even then, African Americans were paid less than whites for the same work and were usually given the lowest jobs.

Enslaved African Americans from the South crossed into Union lines. Many asked to fight against the Confederacy. Instead, the Union hired them as cooks, nurses, porters, and in other tasks. Escaped slaves were classified as property taken in war. Some former slaves were treated well by the Union Army, while others were treated poorly.

In March 1863, the Union allowed African Americans to enlist. The all-black regiments had white officers leading them. The U.S. War Department organized a Bureau of Colored Troops in May 1863. In many battles, African American soldiers proved their bravery. At the battle of Milliken's Bend in Louisiana, African American soldiers who had had less than one month's experience fought against experienced Confederate troops. Three black regiments and one white regiment drove the Confederates out.

Over 175,000 African Americans served in the Union Army. Approximately 29,000 more served in the Union Navy.

Morrill Land Grant Act

The Morrill Land Grant Act of 1862 gave all loyal Union states large pieces of federal land. The states were to use money from the

Song Of The First Arkansas Regiment

This was the song of the 1st Arkansas Regiment, an African American regiment. In 1863, the song was printed in the *Missouri Democrat*, a pro-Union paper. The song was sung to the tune of a well-known song called "The Battle Hymn of the Republic."

Oh! we're the bully soldiers of the First of Arkansas,
We are fighting for the Union, we are fighting for the law;
We can hit a **rebel** further than a white man ever saw.
As we go marching on.
See, there above the center, where the flag is waving bright,
We are going out of slavery, we're bound for freedom's light.
We mean to show **Jeff Davis** how the African can fight,
As we go marching on.
We are done with hoeing cotton, we are done with hoeing corn;
We are colored Yankee soldiers now, as sure as you are born;
When the **massas** hear us yelling, they'll think it's **Gabriel's horn**,
As we go marching on....
We have heard the **proclamation**, massa hush it as he will;
The bird he sing it to us hopping on the cotton hill,
And the 'possum up the gum tree, he couldn't keep it still,
As he went climbing on.
They said, "Now, my colored brethren, you shall be forever free,
From the first of January, eighteen hundred sixty-three."
We heard it in the river going rushing to the sea,
As it went sounding on.
Father Abraham has spoken and the message has been sent,
The prison doors he opened, and out the prisoners went,
To join the sable army of the African descent,
As it goes marching on.
Then fall in, colored brethren, you'd better do it soon,
Don't you hear the drum a-beating the "Yankee Doodle" tune?
We are with you now this morning, we'll be far away at noon,
As we go marching on.

Source: National Society of the Colonial Dames of America.

◀ **rebel**
reference to Confederate soldiers who had "rebelled" against the Union

◀ **Jeff Davis**
Jefferson Davis, the Confederate president

◀ **massa**
master

◀ **Gabriel's horn**
A reference from the Bible to the horn that the prophet Gabriel blows to signal the day that God judges humankind

◀ **proclamation**
the Emancipation Proclamation

◀ **Father Abraham**
Abraham Lincoln

sale of the land to open colleges. These colleges would offer courses in agriculture, engineering, and home economics. The government gave the states a total of 17 million acres. The states earned about $7 million and over 70 colleges were founded. The Morrill Act was extended to the southern states in 1890. The colleges formed there included Alabama A&M and Tuskegee University.

politicians, African American

During the **Reconstruction** (see p. 123) era (1865–1877), African Americans in the South were able to vote for the first time. Nearly all who could vote, did vote. Where African Americans formed the majority, many were elected to federal, state, and local offices. Between 1865 and 1867, there were 20 U.S. congressmen, two U.S. senators, three secretaries of state, a state Supreme Court justice, two state treasurers, and many other public officials. Two African Americans held lieutenant governor positions. Once **Reconstruction** (see p. 123) ended, southern whites took power and African Americans were not allowed to vote.

Hiram Revels became the first African American to serve in the U.S. Senate. He served in the seat that had previously been held by Jefferson Davis, the president of the Confederacy. (Library of Congress)

race riots

Race riots rocked northern and southern cities during and after the **Civil War** (see p. 108). In the North, riots were caused by the passage of the *Conscription* (*con-SKRIP-shun*) Act in March 1863. The act ordered males between the ages of 20 and 46 to report for duty in the Union Army. It allowed people to avoid the draft if they could hire a substitute for $300. Most poor or middle-class whites could not afford to hire substitutes. They were very angry that they were fighting what they called "a rich man's war." Also, many northern whites were against fighting a war to free African Americans. They were concerned that free African Americans would take their jobs away. Riots broke out in Ohio, New York, and other places. The worst riot was the New York City draft riot in July 1863. Rioters attacked African Americans and white abolitionists. About 1,200 people were killed or injured, and $2 million worth of property was damaged. Federal troops were brought in to end the riots.

In 1866 major riots broke out in Louisiana and Tennessee. At least 30 race riots occurred because southern whites tried to stop African Americans from gaining political and economic power.

African Americans in Government

During Reconstruction, African Americans made great strides in government. More than 600 African Americans served in southern state legislatures; 18 held major offices. The list below highlights just a few of the many who gained office.

P. B. S. Pinchback (1837–1921)

Elected lieutenant governor in Louisiana, Pinchback was appointed governor for 43 days after the elected governor was impeached. He was the first African American governor in U.S. history.

Hiram Revels (1822–1901)

A Civil War veteran and minister in the AME church, Revels was elected to the Mississippi Senate in 1869. In 1870, he was elected to the U.S. Senate and became the first African American senator. Because Revels was filling Jefferson Davis's unexpired term, he served only one year.

Blanche K. Bruce (1841–1898)

Born a slave in Virginia, Bruce was freed in 1863 during the Civil War. He was active in promoting and establishing schools for African Americans throughout the war and during Reconstruction. In 1874 he was elected to the U.S. senate, where he served until 1881.

Joseph Rainey (1832–1887)

Rainey was born a slave in South Carolina, but his father purchased his freedom in the 1840s. In 1870, Rainey was elected to Congress, and in 1872 he delivered an address at the Republican National Convention. In 1874, Rainey became the first African American to become Speaker of the House of Representatives.

Robert DeLarge (1842–1874)

Born a slave in South Carolina, DeLarge was elected to the House of Representatives in 1870. The election in which he won his seat was fraught with abuses and irregularities, and neither DeLarge nor his Democratic opponent was seated. DeLarge decided not to run in the next election. However, Alonzo J. Ransier, another African American, won the seat.

Reconstruction

Toward the end of the war, President **Abraham Lincoln** (see pp. 85, 119) had a plan to "reconstruct" the Union, or bringing the Confederacy back into the United States. Before he could put his plan into action, Lincoln was assassinated.

Abraham Lincoln's vice president, Andrew Johnson, took office. Johnson followed Lincoln's plan. The plan made it fairly easy for southern states to rejoin the Union. It also gave white planters the feeling that they could regain their power. Southern governments quickly passed **black codes** (see p. 105). These limited the freedom of African Americans.

Many Republicans saw Johnson's plan as too easy on the South. The Radical Republicans, led by **Thaddeus Stevens** (see p. 125) of Pennsylvania, passed a series of laws that began a period called "Radical Reconstruction." They wanted to punish the South. They began by passing the **Freedmen's Bureau** Act of 1866 (see p. 117) and the Civil Rights Act of 1866 (see p. 107). In 1867, Congress passed the first Reconstruction Act. This law divided the South into five zones controlled by the military. Anyone who had served in the Confederate Army was not allowed to vote. To be readmitted to the Union, the southern states had to ratify the 14th Amendment (See **amendments to the U.S. Constitution**, p. 105).

The following year the Radical Republicans in the House impeached President Andrew Johnson. However, the Senate voted not to remove him from office.

About 1875, Radical Republicans began to lose support. Reconstruction ended with the election of 1876. In that election, Republican Rutherford B. Hayes won fewer popular votes than his Democratic opponent Samuel J. Tilden. However, the vote counts for Louisiana, South Carolina, and Florida were disputed. Each of these states had a Reconstruction government that had little real power. These governments each sent the U.S. Congress one vote count for their states. However, true power in each of these states was held by powerful whites who favored the Democrat Tilden. These men saw that a second set of vote totals was sent to Congress. In the end, Congress voted to accept the count that made Hayes president if Hayes promised to end Reconstruction. Hayes agreed. After this, African Americans lost the right to vote and other civil rights. They would not begin to gain these rights back until the 1960s.

sharecropping system

Sharecropping is a system of farming that developed in the South after the **Civil War** (see p. 108). Landowners would provide land, tools, and seed on credit to farm laborers. The farm workers, called "croppers," would work the land. When the harvest was sold, the cropper and the landowner divided the profits. The cropper would then pay his debts and borrow for the next season.

Sharecropping was a way for landowners to get their land worked without paying wages. This system gave newly freed Africans some independence. In the years just after the Civil War, the system benefited both landowners and croppers. Cotton prices stayed high. Government officials ensured that African Americans were treated fairly. After **Reconstruction** (see p. 123), things changed. With no one to protect their rights, sharecroppers suffered.

Stevens, Thaddeus

Thaddeus Stevens was an antislavery congressman from the state of Pennsylvania. He was first elected to the House of Representatives in 1848. He stayed in Congress until his death. Stevens was against the **Compromise of 1850** (see p. 79), especially the **Fugitive Slave Act** (see p. 56). In 1856, Stevens was reelected as a member of the new **Republican Party** (see p. 87). He led Congress in passing legislation that brought rights to African Americans.

Thaddeus Stevens of Pennsylvania was a leader of the Radical Republicans in Congress after the Civil War. He helped lead the effort to punish the South for the war. (Library of Congress)

United States v. Cruikshank

In 1873, a group of armed white men in Louisiana killed over 100 African Americans during a disputed governor's election. This attack is known as the Colfax Massacre. Three of the white men involved in the massacre were later found guilty of breaking a Reconstruction law known as the Enforcement Act. The law stated that it was illegal to deny the constitutional rights of any citizen.

The men appealed their case to the U.S. Supreme Court. The court ruled that they had not denied any constitutional rights since, it said, "right of suffrage [voting] is not a necessary [component] of national citizenship…the right to vote in the states comes from the states." This meant that only the states could protect voting rights. It also meant that the only the state of Louisiana could decide to punish the men guilty of the Colfax Massacre. Since it was nearly unheard of for a white man to be punished for killing an African American in the South at this time, this court decision was a great blow to African American civil rights.

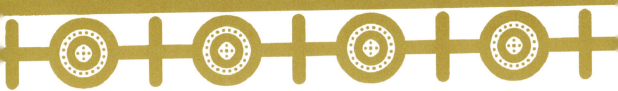

Glossary

alien: a foreign-born resident of a country who has not become a citizen of his or her new country.

appeal: an urgent request, or in legal cases, to make a request that another, higher court hear or review a case that a lower court has already decided in hope of a different outcome.

apprentice: a person who has legally agreed to work for a specific amount of time for a master craftsman in a craft or trade in order to learn that trade.

arsenal: a place for making or storing weapons.

barter: to trade or exchange goods or services in return for other goods or services instead of for money.

blacksmith: a person who works with iron, including someone who makes and fits horseshoes.

cabinet member: A member of a group of advisors to the president, made up of the heads of various government departments.

capital punishment: the penalty of death for committing a crime.

charter: a written grant of rights made to a person, company or other organizations. In the case of colonial America, for example, the English government gave groups and individuals charters to establish colonies in the Americas.

clergy: people ordained for religious services, such as a minister, priest, or rabbi.

conductor: In the case of the Underground Railroad, a "conductor" is a person who led escaped slaves on their journey to freedom.

conscription: the process of signing up

for military service when its ordered by the government instead of voluntary.

Creole: People of mixed European and African ancestry who are descended from the original French settlers of New Orleans.

delegate: a person authorized to speak or act as a representative of others. For example, members of the U.S. Congress are delegates representing the voters of their state or district.

estate: all of a persons land and possessions; *estate* can also refer specifically to the home and surrounding lands that are owned by a wealthy person.

extremist: a person who holds a political view that is far from the center, or most commonly held, opinion.

fugitive: someone who is fleeing from danger, from justice, or from the authorities. A runaway slave, for example, is a fugitive.

griot: a French word for a West African singer and storyteller.

latitude: a distance, measured in degrees north or south from the Earth's equator.

manumission: the act of freeing someone, often one's own slave, from slavery.

maroon: a fugitive African slave or his or her descendants.

mason: a person who works with stone, brick or concrete.

Mecca: the holiest city in the religion of Islam; Mecca is the birthplace of the prophet Mohammed, founder of Islam.

militia: an army made up of ordinary citizens instead of professional soldiers.

missionaries: people sent by officials of a specific religion, often to a foreign land, to seek converts to the religion.

monopoly: exclusive control over a commodity or service that is for sale in a given market. Company's that have monopolies over trade can control the prices charged for that item, for example, since no other competitors exists selling the same product or service.

musket: a type of long-barreled gun used before the invention of the rifle.

narrative: a story, an account, or a tale.

overseer: a person who oversees or watches over the work of others. On slave plantations, the overseer was the person responsible for making sure that enslaved Africans were working as hard as they could. If an overseer felt that a fieldworker was not working his hardest, it was the overseer's job to punish the worker, often with whippings or other forms of violence. For this reason, the overseer was often the most feared person on a plantation.

Parliament: in the case of Great Britain, the Parliament is the country's law-making body, made up of the House of Commons and the House of Lords. The leader of the government, a member of Parliament, is known as the prime minister.

regiment: a type of military unit.

repeal: to withdraw or cancel a previously existing law.

smallpox: an extremely contagious and deadly disease caused by a virus.

sovereign: a ruling person who has power or authority over a country, such as a king.

spirituals: religious hymns sung by African Americans beginning in the 18th and 19th centuries. Spirituals combined both African and European musical styles.

spontaneous: an action that is taken because of a sudden impulse or desire instead of from previous planning.

surveyor: a person who surveys, or gathers information about land, usually by measuring, for the purpose of future building or developing on it.

temperance: avoidance of, or moderation in, drinking alcohol. For example, supporters of the temperance movement in the 19th century were against the drinking of alcohol.

terracotta: a kind of hard, brownish-red clay used for pottery and sculpture.

theology: the study of religion.

treason: a betrayal of one's country or leader, such as one's king. In times of war, for example, giving aid or comfort to the enemy is often thought as an act of treason.

unalienable: incapable of being surrendered or given up, also *inalienable*.

veto: an order prohibiting some proposal or act. In the case of a presidential veto in American politics, the president has the right to refuse to sign bills sent to him by the Congress, thus preventing it from becoming law. Congress can only overturn a veto by the president if two-thirds of the members of both the House of Representatives and Senate vote to overturn the veto.

Resources

General Subjects

BOOKS

Abdul-Jabbar, Kareem, and Alan Steingberg. *Black Profiles in Courage: A Legacy of African-American Achievement*. New York: Morrow, 1996. (Middle School – High School) Read more at Amazon.com.

Altman, Susan. *Encyclopedia of African American Heritage*. 1st Edition. New York: Facts on File, 2001.

Bell, Janet Cheatham. *Stretch Your Wings: Famous Black Quotations for Teens*. New York: Little, Brown & Company, 1999.

Christian, Charles M. and Sari J. Bennett. *Black Saga—The African American Experience: A Chronology*. Baltimore, MD: Counterpoint Press, 1998.

Haber, Louis. *Black Pioneers of Science and Invention*. New York: Harcourt, Brace, & World Inc., 1970.

Hancock, Sibyl. *Famous Firsts of Black Americans*. Gretna, LA: Pelican, 1983.

Hine, Darlene C., and Kathleen Thompson. *Facts on File Encyclopedia of Black Women in America*. New York: Facts on File, 1997.

Hudson, Wade. *Book of Black Heroes: From A to Z: Volume One.* East Orange, NJ: Just Us Books, 1988.

Karenga, Maulana. *Kwanzaa: A Celebration of Family, Community and Culture.* Los Angeles: University of Sankore Press, 1997.

Kranz, Rachel. *The Biographical Dictionary of Black Americans.* New York: Facts of File, 1992.

Myers, Walter Dean. *Now Is Your Time: The African American Struggle for Freedom.* New York: HarperCollins, 1992.

New York Public Library African American Desk Reference. Schomburg Center for Research in Black Culture. New York: Wiley, 1999.

New York Public Library Amazing African American History: A Book of Answers for Kids. New York: Wiley, 1997.

Pinkney, Andrea Davis. *Let It Shine: Stories of Black Women Freedom Fighters.* New York: Harcourt, 2000.

Richardson, Ben Albert. *Great Black Americans.* 2d rev. ed. New York: Crowell, 1976.

Smith, Jesse Carne, ed. *Notable Black American Women.* Third Edition. Detroit, MI: Gale, 2002.

Stewart, Jeffrey C. *1001 Things Everyone Should Know About African American History.* New York: Doubleday, 1997.

Turner, Glennette Tilley. *Follow in Their Footsteps.* New York: Cobblehill Books, 1997.

Yarbrough, Camille. *Cornrows.* New York: Paper Star, 1997.

AUDIO

Every Tone a Testimony: A Smithsonian Folkways African American Aural History. Washington, DC: Smithsonian Folkways Recordings, 2001.

The Long Road to Freedom: An Anthology of Black Music. New York: Buddah, 2001.

Our Souls Have Grown Deep Like the Rivers: Black Poets Read Their Work. Westwood, CA: WEA/Rhino, 2000.

CD-ROM
Encarta Africana Library of Black America. 3rd. ed. Redmond, WA: Microsoft, 2000.

WEBSITES
Africa Online–Africa Kids Only: http://www.africaonline.com/site/africa/kids.jsp

African American History and Culture: http://www.si.edu/resource/faq/nmah/afroam.htm

The African American Journey: http://www2.worldbook.com/students/feature_index.asp

African American Mosaic: http://lcweb.loc.gov/exhibits/african/afam001.html

African American Oddysey: http://memory.loc.gov/ammem/aaohtml/aohome.html

AFROAmeric@ Kid's Zone: http://www.afro.com/kidstalk/

AFRO-American Almanac: http://www.toptags.com/aama/index.htm

Anacostia Museum and Center for African American History and Culture: http://anacostia.si.edu/

Education First Black History Activities: http://www.kn.pacbell.com/wired/BHM/AfroAm.html

Lest We Forget: http://www.coax.net/people/lwf/

National Civil Rights Museum: http://www.civilrightsmuseum.org/

History and Biography

BOOKS

Cox, Clinton. *Undying Glory: The Story of the Massachusetts 54th Regiment.* Mahwah, NJ: Troll Associates, 1999.

Hamilton, Virginia. *Many Thousands Gone: African-Americans from Slavery to Freedom.* New York: Knopf, 2002.

Herda, D.J. *The Dred Scott Case: Slavery and Citizenship.* Berkeley Heights, NJ: Enslow Publishers, 1994.

Levine, Ellen. *Freedom's Children: Young Civil Rights Activists Tell Their Own Stories.* New York: Puffin, 2000.

McKissock, Pat. *Christmas in the Big House, Christmas in the Quarters.* New York: Scholastic, 1994.

Miller, William. *Frederick Douglass: The Last Day of Slavery.* New York: Lee and Low Books, 1999.

Thomas, Velma Maia. *Lest We Forget: The Passage from Africa to Slavery and Emancipation.* New York: Crown Trade Paperbacks, 1997.

VIDEO

Africans in America: America's Journey Through Slavery. New York: PBS Video. 1998.

Black Americans of Achievement: Frederick Douglas. Wynnewood, PA: Schlesinger Media, 1992.

Black Americans of Achievement: Harriet Tubman. Wynnewood, PA: Schlesinger Media, 1992.

Black Americans of Achievement: Sojourner Truth. Wynnewood, PA: Schlesinger Media, 1992.

WEBSITES

Aboard the Underground Railroad: http://www.cr.nps.gov/nr/travel/underground/

African American Military History—The Revolutionary War: http://www.coax.net/people/lwf/rev_war.htm

Africans in America: http://www.pbs.org/wgbh/aia/home.html

Art and Life in Africa: http://www.uiowa.edu/~africart/toc/people.html

Born in Slavery: Slave Narratives from the Federal Writers' Project, 1936-1938: http://memory.loc.gov/ammem/snhtml/snhome.html

Civil War Freedom Fighters: http://www.bjmjr.com/civwar/usct.htm

Excerpts from Slave Narratives: http://vi.uh.edu/pages/mintz/primary.htm

Frederick Douglass Papers at the Library of Congress: http://memory.loc.gov/ammem/doughtml/doughome.html

The Internet African American History Challenge: http://www.brightmoments.com/black-history/

National Underground Railroad Freedom Center: http://www.undergroundrailroad.org/

Slaves and the Courts, 1740-1860: http://memory.loc.gov/ammem/sthtml/sthome.html

The Underground Railroad: http://www.coax.net/people/lwf/undrgrnd.htm

Folklore, Fiction and Poetry

BOOKS

Hamilton, Virginia. *The People Could Fly: The Book of Black Folktales.* New York: Random House, 2000.

Hudson, Wade, and Cheryl Willis Hudson. *In Praise of Our Fathers and Our Mothers: A Black Family Treasury by Outstanding Authors and Artists*. East Orange, NJ: Just Us Books, 1997.

Hughes, Langston. *The Block: Poems*. New York: Viking, 1995.

Lester, Julius. *The Tales of Uncle Remus: The Adventures of B'rer Rabbit*. New York: Puffin, 1999.

McKissock, Pat. *The Dark-Thirty: Southern Tales of the Supernatural*. New York: Knopf, 1996.

Myers, Walter Dean. *Monster*. New York: Harper Collins, 1999.

Rollins, Charlemae Hill, ed. *Christmas Gif': An Anthology of Christmas Poems, Songs, and Stories Written by and About African-Americans*. New York: Morrow Junior Books, 1993.

Selected Bibliography

Andrews, William L., and Henry Lewis Gates Jr. *Slave Narratives*. New York: Library of America, 2000.

Appiah, Kwame Anthony, and Henry Lewis Gates Jr. *Africana: The Encyclopedia of the African and African American Experience*. New York: Basic Civitas Books, 1999.

Barbeau, Arthur, and Florette Henri. *The Unknown Soldiers: African American Troops in World War I*. New York: Da Capo, 1996.

Bennett, Lerone, Jr. *Pioneers in Protest*. Chicago: Johnson Publishing, 1968.

Berlin, Ira. *Many Thousands Gone: The First Two Centuries of Slavery in North America*. Cambridge, MA: Harvard University Press, 2000.

Branch, Taylor. *Parting the Waters*. New York: Simon & Schuster, 1989.

———. *Pillar of Fire*. New York: Simon & Schuster, 1998.

Cowan, Tom, and Jack Maguire. *Timelines of African-American History: Five Hundred Years of Black Achievement*. New York: Berkley Publishing Group, 1994.

DjeDje, Jacqueline Cogdell. *Turn Up the Volume!: A Celebration of African Music*. Berkeley: University of California Press, 1998.

Dodd, Donald. *Historical Statistics of the United States*. Westport, CT: Greenwood Publishing Group, Inc., 1993.

Du Bois, W. E. B. *Souls of Black Folk*. New York: NAL/Dutton, 1995.

Finkelman, Paul. *Slavery in the Courtroom: An Annotated Bibliography of American Cases*. Washington: Lawbook Exchange, 1996.

Foner, Eric. *Reconstruction*. New York: HarperCollins, 1989.

Garrow, David. *Bearing the Cross: Martin Luther King, Jr. and the Southern Christian Leadership Conference, 1955–1968*. New York: William Morrow, 1999.

Harley, Sharon. *The Timetables of African-American History*. New York: Simon & Schuster, 1995.

Hughes, Langston, et al. *A Pictorial History of African Americans*, 6th ed. New York: Crown Publishing, 1995.

Kelley, Robin D. G., and Earl Lewis. *To Make Ourselves Anew: A History of African Americans*. New York: Oxford University Press, 2000.

McPherson, James. *Ordeal by Fire: The Civil War and Reconstruction*. New York: Knopf, 1992.

Peterson, Robert W. *Only the Ball Was White*. Oxford: Oxford University Press, 1992.

Ploski, Harry, and James Williams, eds. *Encyclopedia of African-American History*. New York: Macmillan Library Reference USA, 1996.

Schubert, Frank. *Black Valor: Buffalo Soldiers and the Medal of Honor, 1870–1898*. Wilmington, DE: Scholarly Resources, 1997.

Smith, Carter, ed. *The Black Experience*. New York: Facts On File, Inc., 1990.

Thomas, Velma Maia. *Freedom's Children: The Passage from Emancipation to the Great Migration*. New York: Crown Publishing, 2000.

U.S. Census Bureau. Annual Yearbook. Washington, DC: Government Printing Office, 1996.

——. Reports. Washington, DC: Government Printing Office, 1900, 1910, 1920, 1930, 1940, 1950.

Index

Note: The index below contains entries for both volumes of the Student Almanac of African American History. The roman numeral I refers to pages in the first volume. The roman numeral II refers to pages in the second volume.

A

Abolitionists, I: 32, 44, 45, 55, 65, 67, 73, 76, 77, 80, 82, 83, 84, 85, 88, 90, 99; II: 12

Abyssinian Baptist Church, II: 43, 45

affirmative action, II: 99, 105, 125

African American studies, II: 101, 105

African art and culture (to the 1500s), I: 19, 21

African Colonization Society, I: 43, 65, 73, 84

African kingdoms, I: 11, 19

African Methodist Episcopal Church, I: 9, 46, 47; II: 31

Africanus, Leo, I: 11, 21

Allen, Richard, I: 9, 40, 46, 56, 57, 62, 74

amendments to the U.S. Constitution, I: 101, 105, 107, 124

American Missionary Association, I: 105, 111

American Revolution, I: 8, 38, 40, 45, 47, 49, 51, 53, 56

Amistad, I: 68, 69, 75

Amos 'n' Andy, II: 41, 45

apartheid, II: 102, 106

Armstrong, Louis, II: 42, 45, 47, 58

Articles of Confederation of the United Colonies of New England, The, I: 16, 21

arts and literature, II: 13, 19, 42, 45, 58

Attucks, Crispus, I: 40, 47, 49, 51

B

Banneker, Benjamin, I: 41, 49

Baptist Church, I: 18, 46, 49

Basie, William "Count," II: 45, 48

Beckwourth, James, I: 70, 76, 95

Bethune, Mary McLeod, II: 43, 48

Birmingham, Alabama, II: 72, 73, 77, 83, 84

Black Cabinet, II: 43, 49

Black Codes, I: 16, 22, 24, 100, 101, 105, 124

Black Panther Party, II: 75, 76, 79, 81, 95

Black Power, II: 75, 76, 79, 80, 93, 95

Boston Massacre, I: 38, 49, 51

Brotherhood of Sleeping Car Porters, II: 44, 50

Brown v. *Board of Education*, II: 9, 61, 70, 71, 81, 85, 90, 99

Brown, John, I: 72, 76

Brownsville Affair, II: 39, 51

Buffalo Soldiers, II: 12, 20

Burns, Anthony, I: 77

business, African Americans in, II: 99, 104, 106,

Busing, II: 99, 107, 110

Byrd William, II, I: 16, 18, 22, 50

C

Calhoun, John C., I: 70, 77

Carver, George Washington, II: 17, 29, 51

Chicago Defender, II: 39, 52,

Civil Rights Act of 1964, II: 72, 76, 82

civil rights acts, I: 102, 107

Civil Rights Cases, II: 14, 21, 24

Civil Rights Restoration Act, II: 99, 108

Civil War, I: 71, 96, 97, 98, 108, 110, 111, 113, 115, 117, 118, 119, 120, 122, 124; II: 7, 12, 19, 20, 22, 28, 30, 38, 116

Coffin, Levi, I: 79, 91

Compromise of 1850, I: 70, 79, 125

Confederate States of America, I: 10, 97, 98, 108, 110, 111; II: 16

Confiscation Acts, I: 98, 109, 110

Congress of Racial Equality (CORE), II: 70, 81, 82

Coppin, Fanny Jackson, I: 110, 112

Cotton Club, II: 42, 52, 52, 58

cotton gin, I: 9, 43, 51, 60

Cuffe, Paul, I: 9, 39, 52, 74

D

Davis, Jefferson, I: 110, 111

Declaration of Independence, I: 9, 38, 53

Douglass, Frederick, I: 10, 68, 73, 80, 82, 83, 88; II: 19

Drew, Charles, II: 43, 52

Du Bois, William Edward Burghardt, II: 8, 16, 20, 22, 38, 39, 47, 53, 62, 63

Du Sable, Jean-Baptiste Point, I: 39, 54

E

education, I: 102, 105, 111, 117; II: 22, 55, 108

election of 1876, II: 11, 22

Emancipation Proclamation, I: 86, 99, 113, 120; II: 20

Equal Employment Opportunity Act, II: 110

Equiano, Olaudah, I: 40, 54

Estevanico, I: 11, 22

Exodusters, II: 8, 13, 14, 15, 22

F

Fisk Jubilee Singers, I: 105, 115

Fort Pillow Massacre, I: 100, 115, 118

Forten, Charlotte, **I:** 99, 115
Forten, James, **I:** 41, 56, 73, 74, 115
"forty acres and a mule," **I:** 101, 116
Free African Society, **I:** 40, 47, 56
free blacks, **I:** 9, 16, 23, 25, 49, 56, 66, 91, 96; **II:** 14
Free Soil Party, **I:** 69, 73, 82, 87
Freedmen's Bureau, **I:** 101, 102, 112, 117, 124
Freedmen's Village, **I:** 102, 117
Freedom Rides, **II:** 70, 72, 82, 94
Freedom Summer, **II:** 83, 94
Freeman Field Mutiny, **II:** 44, 56
French and Indian War, **I:** 17, 25, 37
Fugitive Slave Act, **I:** 56, 62, 70, 77, 79, 82, 125

G
Garnet, Henry Highland, **I:** 69, 83; **II:** 20
Garrison, William Lloyd, **I:** 67, 68, 73, 81, 84
Garvey, Marcus, **II:** 40, 56
Germantown, **I:** 15, 25
Great Migration, **II:** 39, 52, 55, 57, 64
Greeley, Horace, **I:** 103, 117

H
Hale, Clara McBride, **II:** 104, 110
Harlem Renaissance, **II:** 9, 42, 47, 58
hate crimes, **II:** 102, 103, 111
health, African American, **II:** 112
Houston Mutiny, **II:** 40, 58

I
immigration, African and Caribbean, **II:** 113

indentured servants, **I:** 8, 15, 25

J
Jackson, Jesse, **II:** 100, 114
Jamestown, **I:** 8, 13, 15, 25
jazz, **II:** 39, 40, 45, 58, 117
Jim Crow laws, **II:** 8, 13, 17, 24, 37, 40, 82, 91, 92
Johnson, Anthony, **I:** 15, 26
Jones, Absalom, **I:** 40, 47, 56, 62

K
Kansas-Nebraska Act, **I:** 71, 77, 85
Kemble, Frances Anne (Fanny), **I:** 100, 118
Key, Elizabeth, **I:** 14, 27
King, Martin Luther, Jr., **II:** 10, 71, 72, 73, 74, 75, 77, 84, 89, 91, 92, 95, 100, 115
Knights of Labor, **II:** 12, 24
Ku Klux Klan, **I:** 101, 103, 115, 118; **II:** 37

L
L'Ouverture, Toussaint, **I:** 41, 58
Las Casas, Bartolomé de, **I:** 13, 28
Lincoln, Abraham, **I:** 10, 72, 81, 85, 87, 97, 99, 108, 113, 117, 119, 120, 123; **II:** 11, 85, 119
literature, African Americans in, **II:** 100, 104, 115
Little Rock, Arkansas, **II:** 71, 72, 82, 85
Los Angeles Riots, **II:** 101, 102, 116
Louisiana Purchase, **I:** 44, 57
Louisiana Territory, **I:** 42, 57, 58
lynchings, **II:** 11, 25, 38

M

Malcolm X, II: 10, 62, 70, 74, 76, 79, 87, 102, 124

March on Washington, II: 44, 50, 60, 73, 75, 84, 89, 94

Margold Report, II: 42, 61

Marshall, Thurgood, II: 70, 81, 89, 103, 125

Massachusetts Body of Liberties, I: 14, 29

Mather, Cotton, I: 15, 30

Middle Passage, I: 14, 30

military, African Americans in, I: 120

Million Man March, II: 102, 103, 117, 124

minstrel shows, I: 68, 86; II: 17, 19

Missouri Compromise, I: 9, 44, 57, 58, 65

Montgomery Bus Boycott, II: 71, 84, 90

Morrill Land Grant Act, I: 99, 120

music, African Americans in, II: 104, 117

N

Nation of Islam, II: 42, 61, 70, 87, 101, 117, 124

National Association for the Advancement of Colored People (NAACP), II: 9, 39, 53, 55, 61, 62, 64, 70, 74, 81, 90, 91, 117

National Association of Colored Women, II: 18, 26

negro league, II: 42, 62

New Deal, II: 42, 50, 62

Niagara Movement, II: 39, 55, 63

Northup, Solomon, I: 86, 88

Northwest Ordinance, I: 58

P

Plessy v. Ferguson, II: 8, 17, 18, 26, 70, 81

politicians, African American, I: 102, 103, 122

politics, African Americans in, II: 98, 99, 102, 118

Populist Party, II: 16, 17, 27

Powell, Colin, II: 104, 120

Prosser, Gabriel, I: 58

Q

Quakers, I: 18, 30, 45, 52

R

race riots, I: 99, 100, 101, 122; II: 101, 116, 122

Reconstruction, I: 101, 104, 105, 107, 111, 112, 119, 122, 123, 125; II: 11, 13, 22, 25, 118, 123

Red Summer, II: 41, 64

religion, I: 20, 32, 50, 66

Republican Party, I: 73, 87, 117, 125

Robinson, Jackie, II: 9, 62, 70, 91, 93

Royal African Company, I: 15, 33

S

science and technology, II: 14, 28

Scott, Dred, I: 71, 81

Scottsboro Boys, II: 41, 65

Seminole Wars, I: 43, 59

sharecropping, I: 104, 124; II: 8, 13, 29

sit-in, II: 70, 92

slave laws, I: 34

slave narratives, I: 87, 88

slave revolts, I: 33, 34

slavery, I: 60, 88

Southern Christian Leadership Conference (SCLC), **II:** 71, 72, 77, 81, 84, 92, 95, 115, 118

sports, African Americans in, **II:** 16, 76, 30, 93, 99, 100, 102, 103, 120

Stevens, Thaddeus, **I:** 101, 124, 125

Stono rebellion, **I:** 40

Strauder v. *West Virginia*, **II:** 14, 30

Student Nonviolent Coordinating Committee (SNCC), **II:** 72, 73, 80, 92, 93, 95, 96

T

television and film, African Americans in, **II:** 100, 101, 102, 104, 122

Terrell, Mary Church, **II:** 31

Thomas, Clarence, **II:** 101, 103, 124

triangle trade, **I:** 14, 30, 34

Truth, Sojourner, **I:** 10, 68, 69, 89

Tubman, Harriet, **I:** 10, 70, 71, 89, 93, 99

Tulsa Riot, **II:** 41, 66

Turner, Nat, **I:** 66, 67, 90

Tuskegee Institute, **II:** 14, 17, 31, 38

U

U.S. Constitution, **I:** 9, 43, 56, 62, 106

U.S. Civil War **I:** 8, 10, 108; **II:** 13, 16, 26, 28, 32

Uncle Tom's Cabin, **I:** 90

Underground Railroad, **I:** 67, 76, 79, 90, 91, 99

United States v. *Cruikshank*, **I:** 104, 125

V

Vesey Conspiracy, **I:** 66, 92

Virginia House of Burgesses, **I:** 35

Voting Rights Act of 1965, **II:** 74, 95

W

Walker, David, **I:** 66, 93

Wallace, George, **II:** 76, 96

War of 1812, **I:** 9, 43, 56, 62

Washington, Booker T., **II:** 14, 17, 32, 38, 48, 51, 63

Wells, Ida B., **II:** 17, 34

West Indies, **I:** 14, 35, 54, 55

Wheatley, Phillis, **I:** 39, 63

World War I, **II:** 9, 39, 40, 55, 57, 67

World War II, **II:** 9, 43, 44, 52, 55, 56, 57, 67, 69